Graceful Transitions: Navigating the Journey With Aging Parents

Compassionate Guidance for Caring Relationships: A Practical Handbook for Supporting Aging Parents With Dignity and Respect

By SB Wade

Table of Contents

Introduction

"The affection and support we offer our aging parents are among the most cherished aspects of our existence" (Mancini & Blieszner, 1989). It's a journey marked by tender moments and shared memories, but it's also one fraught with challenges and heartaches that can leave us feeling overwhelmed, helpless, and in desperate need of guidance. If you're reading these words, you've likely embarked on this poignant voyage, and you've felt the weight of the responsibilities, uncertainties, and profound love that accompanies caring for aging parents.

Picture this: A quiet evening, the phone rings, and your heart skips a beat as you see your parent's name on the caller ID. You answer, and the voice on the other end sounds fragile, a stark contrast to the once-strong figure you've always known. It's a moment of realization—the catalyst that brought you here, to this book. You understand that this journey is more than just aging; it involves a balance of compassion and respect, a path that deserves nothing less than graceful guidance.

The Benefits Await You

In *Graceful Transitions: Navigating the Journey with Aging Parents*, we offer you a roadmap through the complexities of caregiving and aging. We understand the painful challenges you face, and we're here to provide solutions that will bring clarity, relief, and peace of mind.

As you read through these pages, you will discover:

- A checklist of important legal documents your parent should secure before it's too late, saving you from future legal turmoil.

- Compassionate guidance on addressing sensitive and emotional topics that you and your parent need to discuss urgently, no matter how uncomfortable they may be.

- Strategies for dealing with stubbornness and denial when your parent resists help, ensuring their well-being.

- Seven self-care techniques to help you combat caregiver burnout, preserving your own physical and emotional health.

- Insights into the challenges and expectations of being a caregiver for an elderly parent, offering you support on this demanding journey.

- A guide to the five stages of grief to help you decipher and understand your emotions, making space for healing.

- Over 20 meaningful ways to celebrate your parent's legacy, honoring their life and the love you share.

Real Stories, Real Results

This book is not just a collection of words; it's a lifeline. You'll find extreme testimonials of real people who have applied these principles to their lives and achieved remarkable transformations. Celebrities, like the well-known Queen

Latifah, have openly shared their experiences of finding solace, confidence, and fulfillment through the wisdom contained within these pages.

Queen Latifah cared for her terminally ill mother while keeping her acting career going. She admits that it was tough and it was very easy to lose oneself in the situation. She recommends that if you, the caregiver, are not looking after yourself, you can't do a good job of looking after the patient. Give yourself a break to spoil yourself with a nap, a walk, or time to read a book. Once you are refreshed, you can give time to your loved one with a positive attitude.

Maria Shriver took care of her father during his last days with Alzheimer's disease. She opened up about the mixed feelings that caregivers have. There is the willingness to care for the loved one but sneaking in under these feelings is a feeling of guilt that you don't really want to take on this time-consuming job. This is known as caregiver guilt. You can love the person but hate the challenges that caregiving brings. She advises that you do the best that you can for the person and that you look after yourself.

Peter Gallagher cared for his mother when she was diagnosed with Alzheimer's. He revealed that the diagnosis was just as bad for a carer as it was for the patient. He cared for his mother for more than 20 years.

Amy Grant and her sisters cared for both of their parents, who had been diagnosed with dementia. She emphasizes the importance of caregivers having a support network, as this role is too demanding to manage without help.

Henry Winkler and his sister jointly cared for their mom when she suffered a debilitating stroke. He acknowledges that a caregiver's job is difficult and that caregivers deserve hero's status.

There are many other celebrities who have taken on caring for a parent. To name a few:

- The Baldwin brothers cared for their mother, who had breast cancer.

- Rob Lowe cared for his father.

- Dwayne "The Rock" Johnson cared for his mother, who had lung cancer.

- Patrick Dempsey cared for his mother, who had ovarian cancer.

The End Result

Imagine a life where you confidently address the challenges of caring for aging parents. Picture yourself having those difficult conversations with grace, knowing you're providing the best possible care. Envision a future where you cherish your time together, unburdened by stress and burnout, and celebrate your parent's legacy with deep appreciation and love.

Why Trust Us?

As the author of this book, I'm not just an observer; I've walked the same path you're on. I've faced the uncertainties, the sleepless nights, and the heart-wrenching decisions. I know firsthand how difficult it was before having the "new" information that I'm about to share with you. My mission is to empower you with knowledge, insights, and strategies to make this journey smoother, more meaningful, and, ultimately, a beautiful expression of love.

This Is the Right Book for You

If you're seeking a guide that combines practical wisdom, heartfelt stories, and proven strategies, you're in the right place. *Graceful Transitions* is more than a book; it's a companion, a source of strength, and a beacon of hope on your journey with aging parents. Together, let's embark on this transformational voyage, where grace and dignity light the way.

Chapter 1:

Our Journey With Aging Parents: Roles and Expectations

"Age is an issue of mind over matter.
If you don't mind, it doesn't matter."
— Mark Twain

Welcome to the journey of understanding the profound changes that aging parents undergo and your evolving role as a caregiver. In this chapter, we'll examine the physical, emotional, and cognitive transformations that aging brings, equipping you with insights to travel this path with empathy and grace.

Embracing the Aging Process

Aging is a fundamental part of life, marked by a series of changes and experiences that unfold over time. To support your parents in their aging journey, it's important to gain a deep understanding of it through scientific insights. This knowledge will empower you to approach this journey with readiness and acceptance.

Aging is not a solitary event, but rather a lifelong journey filled with various chapters, each marked by its unique challenges and joys. It's an accumulation of wisdom, resilience, and a lifetime of memories. Understanding the complexities of this journey, from physical changes to emotional shifts and cognitive alterations, equips you with the tools to provide compassionate care and support.

Approaching the aging process with knowledge and empathy allows you to celebrate the moments of triumph and navigate the inevitable hurdles with grace and understanding. It offers an opportunity to strengthen the bonds with your aging parents and cherish the time you spend together. By embracing the aging process as an integral part of the human experience, you embark on a path of caregiving that is not only fulfilling but also deeply enriching.

Armed with a profound understanding of aging, you are better prepared to provide the unwavering support and respect that your parents deserve as they traverse this remarkable journey.

Physical Changes

Medical Conditions

Aging often comes with an increased vulnerability to chronic health conditions and a worsening of existing ones. Conditions such as diabetes, hypertension, arthritis, or heart disease may become more prevalent or harder to manage as one ages. What might have been manageable in the past with minimal medical intervention could now demand more attention, including regular doctor visits, medication management, and lifestyle adjustments. These changes may require a higher level of medical care and oversight, potentially impacting your aging parent's daily routine and healthcare regimen.

Mobility

Over time, the ability to move and manage one's environment can gradually decline. Mobility challenges may arise due to factors like muscle weakness, joint stiffness, or balance issues. Your aging parent might find it more challenging to perform activities they once took for granted, such as walking, climbing stairs, or even getting in and out of a chair or their bed. These mobility limitations can significantly impact their daily life, making it essential to create a safe and accessible living environment and possibly explore mobility aids or physical therapy to maintain their independence.

Physical Capabilities

Fine motor skills, speed, reflexes, and physical strength can all diminish with age. Fine motor skills, which involve precise movements of the hands and fingers, may decline, affecting tasks like buttoning a shirt, writing, or using utensils. Slower reaction times and reduced reflexes can make activities that require quick responses, such as catching a falling object or avoiding obstacles, more challenging. Additionally, decreased physical strength may limit their ability to lift objects, carry groceries, or perform household chores. These changes in physical capabilities can lead to a reduced sense of independence and may necessitate adaptations or assistance to ensure their safety and well-being.

The physical changes associated with aging can have a significant impact on your aging parent's overall well-being and independence. Recognizing these changes early and addressing them with appropriate medical care, mobility support, and lifestyle adjustments can help maintain their quality of life and ensure their safety as they navigate the aging process.

As you embark on this caregiving journey, it is essential to gain a deep awareness of the common physical changes that aging parents may undergo. This understanding forms the foundation for providing the utmost care and support to ensure their health and well-being:

- **Vision loss:** Vision loss is a common age-related health issue, affecting an estimated one in three elderly individuals (Quillen, 1999). Conditions like macular degeneration, glaucoma, and cataracts become increasingly prevalent as people age, often resulting in impaired vision or blindness. Loss of vision not only reduces quality of life but also poses safety risks, such as increased likelihood of falls or accidents.

  Moreover, it can lead to social isolation and contribute to mental health issues like depression. Despite the availability of corrective procedures and assistive technologies, access to adequate eye care remains a challenge for many seniors, making vision loss an important public health concern that requires more focused attention in geriatric care.

- **Bladder control:** Bladder control issues, commonly referred to as urinary incontinence, are a frequent concern among the elderly. The prevalence of incontinence increases with age and can significantly affect an individual's quality of life, leading to social withdrawal and increased risk of falls due to urgency.

  Contributing factors often include weakened pelvic muscles, prostate enlargement in men, and the effects of medications or chronic illnesses. Despite its impact, many seniors are reluctant to discuss the issue with healthcare providers due to embarrassment or stigma. Effective treatments, ranging from pelvic floor exercises to medications and surgical interventions, are available, but early diagnosis and treatment are key to managing the condition successfully.

- **Hearing loss:** Hearing loss is a prevalent issue among the elderly, affecting approximately one in three people between the ages of 65 and 74, and nearly half of those older than 75, according to the National Institute on Aging (2020). This age-related hearing loss, known as presbycusis, can significantly impact quality of life, leading to social isolation, depression, and even cognitive decline.

  Despite its prevalence, hearing loss is often underdiagnosed and undertreated in this population. Hearing aids and other assistive devices can help, but they are not universally accessible due to cost and stigma associated with their use. Consequently, hearing loss remains a critical public health concern requiring greater attention and targeted interventions in geriatric care.

- **Dental health:** Dental health in the elderly is a crucial but often overlooked aspect of overall well-being. Aging is associated with a variety of oral health issues, including gum disease, tooth decay, and tooth loss. Poor oral health can have a significant impact on quality of life, affecting the ability to chew and speak, and can also be linked to other serious health conditions like heart disease.

Regular dental check-ups are vital for early detection and treatment of problems, yet many seniors face barriers to dental care, such as lack of insurance or physical difficulties in accessing dental services. Therefore, dental health remains an important focus for healthcare providers and caregivers in geriatric care.

- **Digestive issues:** As people age, changes in the digestive system are common and can lead to various bowel problems including constipation, diarrhea, and increased sensitivity to certain foods. Reduced muscle tone in the digestive tract, decreased production of digestive enzymes, and slower transit time for food can all contribute to these issues. Medication side effects and decreased physical activity further exacerbate these problems.

  Gastrointestinal issues in the elderly not only impact quality of life but can also lead to nutritional deficiencies and complicate the management of chronic conditions like diabetes or heart disease. Consequently, addressing digestive and bowel problems is an important aspect of geriatric healthcare.

- **Bone health:** Weaker and more brittle bones are often associated with aging, increased risk of sustaining fractures with falling. Falling is a significant health concern among the elderly, posing a risk for both physical injury and decreased quality of life. According to the U.S. Center for Disease Control and Prevention (CDC), one in four Americans aged 65 and older falls each year, making falls the leading cause of both fatal and non-fatal injuries in this age group (2019). In addition to fractures, falls can result in head injuries and other serious conditions that often lead to hospitalization.

Moreover, the psychological impact of a fall can lead to fear and decreased mobility, further compounding health risks. The financial toll is also significant, with the CDC estimating that the medical costs for falls totaled more than $50 billion in 2015 (2019). Thus, fall prevention and bone health maintenance are a critical area of focus for healthcare providers and caregivers alike.

- **Muscle changes**: Muscle mass and strength tend to decrease with age, a condition known as sarcopenia. Starting around the age of 30, people can lose as much as 3% to 5% of their muscle mass per decade, and this rate accelerates after age 60 (Henry Ford Health, 2023). The loss of muscle mass can have significant consequences for the elderly, including reduced mobility, increased risk of falls, and a general decline in functional independence.

  Muscle weakness is also associated with other health problems, such as insulin resistance and decreased bone density, making it a multi-faceted issue in geriatric care. Exercise programs that include resistance training are the primary method of combating age-related muscle loss, but proper nutrition and medical interventions are also essential components of managing this common age-related change.

- **Cardiovascular changes:** Cardiovascular changes are an inevitable aspect of aging, leading to increased susceptibility to heart-related health issues among the elderly. As people age, their blood vessels stiffen, heart walls thicken, and the heart's ability to pump blood efficiently declines. These changes can contribute to high blood pressure (hypertension), reduced cardiac output, and an elevated risk of developing heart diseases such as coronary artery disease or heart failure.

Moreover, the elderly are more prone to arrhythmias and have a less robust response to sudden cardiac stress, such as during a heart attack. The age-related decline in cardiovascular function underscores the importance of regular medical check-ups, lifestyle modifications, and medication management in preserving heart health and reducing morbidity and mortality in the older population.

- **Decreased endurance:** Decreased endurance is a common issue in the elderly, often attributed to a combination of factors such as reduced cardiovascular efficiency, muscle loss, and metabolic changes. This decline in endurance can severely impact an older individual's ability to perform daily activities and engage in physical exercise, leading to a cycle of reduced physical activity and further endurance loss.

  Diminished endurance also increases the risk of falls and contributes to a greater susceptibility to fatigue, both of which can compromise overall well-being and independence. Interventions like regular, moderate exercise and proper nutrition can help mitigate some of these effects, but decreased endurance remains a significant challenge in geriatric care, requiring tailored healthcare strategies.

- **Medications:** Medication management is a complex and critical issue in geriatric care, as the elderly are often prescribed multiple medications for various chronic conditions. Polypharmacy, the concurrent use of multiple medications, is common among older adults and increases the risk of drug interactions, side effects, and adverse events like falls or hospitalization.

  Age-related changes in metabolism and organ function can also affect how medications are processed, making older individuals more susceptible to overdose or toxicity. Furthermore, cognitive decline can lead to difficulties in managing medication regimens, contributing to non-adherence and potentially exacerbating health issues. Therefore, regular medication reviews and close monitoring by healthcare providers are essential to optimize therapeutic outcomes and minimize risks associated with medication use in the elderly.

By recognizing and acknowledging these common physical changes, you are better equipped to provide the necessary care, support, and adaptations to help your aging parents navigate these transitions with dignity and comfort. It is a crucial step toward ensuring their well-being and improving their overall quality of life as they age.

Cognitive Changes: Addressing the Challenges With Empathy

As our parents gracefully age, it becomes paramount to recognize the cognitive shifts that may transpire. Understanding these changes not only equips you to provide the appropriate support but also enables you to approach caregiving with patience, empathy, and an unwavering commitment to preserving their dignity.

Common Cognitive and Mental Changes

- **Short and long-term memory:** Aging often ushers in noticeable changes in short-term memory, making it more challenging for your parents to remember recent events or details. However, it's crucial to note that long-term memory tends to decline less with age. While they may have difficulty recalling what they had for breakfast, they can vividly recall cherished memories from their youth.

- **Difficulty with recall:** Your aging parents may find themselves grappling with information retrieval, even if it is safely stored in their long-term memory. This struggle with recall can lead to moments of frustration and confusion, as they may recognize the knowledge but find it temporarily inaccessible.

- **Confusion and getting lost:** Aging parents may become easily disoriented about their surroundings, occasionally forgetting their current location or losing track of ongoing events. This can be particularly distressing for them and necessitates a patient and supportive approach.

- **Rational and logical thought:** Cognitive changes can impact judgment and decision-making. Your parents may become more susceptible to scams, make impulse purchases, or arrive at decisions that may appear irrational. Understanding that these shifts are not deliberate, but a result of aging is essential in maintaining a harmonious relationship.

- **Management and organizational abilities:** Aging parents may experience a decline in their capacity to manage tasks and stay organized, even in activities they once handled effortlessly. Simple daily activities may become increasingly challenging, requiring your understanding and assistance.

Recognizing these cognitive changes is not only vital but also an act of profound compassion. It allows you to approach caregiving with a deep reservoir of patience and adaptability, ensuring that your parents receive the unwavering support they need to manage these transitions with grace and dignity.

Emotional Changes: Managing the Depths of Aging

In addition to the cognitive changes we've explored, it's essential to recognize that aging parents may also undergo profound emotional shifts. These emotional transitions can significantly influence both their well-being and your caregiving journey, calling for a compassionate and understanding approach.

- **Anxiety:** Anxiety in the elderly is a common but often overlooked mental health issue that can significantly impair quality of life. The causes can be multifaceted, ranging from chronic medical conditions and medication side effects to life changes such as retirement, loss of a spouse, or increased physical limitations. Symptoms of anxiety might also mimic or exacerbate other age-related health issues, making diagnosis more challenging.

The consequences of untreated anxiety are substantial, including sleep disturbances, decreased physical resilience, and a heightened risk of cardiac issues. Anxiety can also lead to a cycle of reduced social engagement and increased isolation. Proper diagnosis and treatment, typically involving cognitive behavioral therapy, medication, or a combination of both, are vital to managing anxiety symptoms and improving overall well-being in the elderly population.

- **Geriatric depression:** In a later chapter, we will examine the topic of geriatric depression in greater detail. Depression in the elderly is a serious and often underdiagnosed condition that can significantly impact quality of life. While aging naturally brings about life changes that may trigger feelings of sadness or nostalgia, clinical depression is a more severe and persistent problem that requires medical intervention.

Factors contributing to depression in older adults may include chronic illness, medication side effects, loss of loved ones, and social isolation. Depression in this age group is particularly concerning as it increases the risk of physical illnesses, impairs functional abilities, and is associated with higher rates of mortality (Chand & Arif,

2023). Additionally, it can often be misattributed to other aging-related conditions or overlooked due to the stigma surrounding mental health. Proper diagnosis and treatment, often involving a combination of medication and psychotherapy, are crucial for improving well-being and overall health in elderly individuals experiencing depression.

- **Mood swings:** Mood swings in the elderly can be a cause for concern, as they may signify underlying physical or psychological issues. While some level of mood variability is normal at any age, abrupt or severe mood changes in older adults can be symptomatic of health conditions such as hormonal imbalances, nutritional deficiencies, or chronic pain.

  Additionally, mental health issues like depression and anxiety are often underdiagnosed in this population and can manifest as mood swings. Cognitive impairments, such as those seen in Alzheimer's disease or other forms of dementia, can also lead to unpredictable emotional states. Medication interactions or side effects are another common culprit. Because mood swings can have a significant impact on an elderly individual's quality of life and may signal other health issues, they warrant thorough medical evaluation and targeted treatment plans.

- **Reluctance to socialize:** Reluctance to socialize is a common issue among the elderly, and it can be triggered by various factors including physical limitations, sensory impairments like vision or hearing loss, and psychological conditions such as depression or anxiety. This withdrawal from social activities can perpetuate a cycle of isolation, leading to further emotional distress and potential cognitive decline.

Additionally, the fear of falling or experiencing incontinence in public can discourage older adults from leaving their homes, reducing opportunities for social interaction. The consequences of social withdrawal are far-reaching, affecting not only emotional well-being but also physical health, as social engagement is linked to better cardiovascular, immune, and cognitive functions (Umberson & Karas Montez, 2010). Addressing the underlying causes of social reluctance is crucial in geriatric care to promote a healthier, more fulfilling life for the elderly.

- **Irrational anger and irritation:** Irrational anger and irritation in the elderly can sometimes be indicative of underlying issues, ranging from physical health problems to emotional distress or cognitive decline. Conditions such as chronic pain, medication side effects, or sleep disturbances can contribute to mood swings and increased irritability.

  Additionally, mental health conditions like depression and anxiety, which are often underdiagnosed in the elderly, can manifest as irritability or anger. Cognitive impairments, such as those seen in Alzheimer's disease and other forms of dementia, can also result in behavioral changes including irritability and aggression. Given the complexity of these emotional changes and the potential for significant impact on quality of life for both the elderly individual and their caregivers, a thorough medical and psychological evaluation is often necessary for effective diagnosis and management.

- **Loneliness:** Loneliness is a significant concern among the elderly, often exacerbated by factors such as the loss of a spouse, social isolation, and limited mobility. Studies indicate that loneliness can have severe health implications, comparable to the risks associated with smoking, obesity, and physical inactivity (CDC, 2021). It can lead to increased levels of stress hormones, poorer cardiovascular function, and a weakened immune system.

  Moreover, loneliness is closely linked to mental health problems like depression and anxiety, and it has been associated with cognitive decline and an increased risk of Alzheimer's disease (CDC, 2019). Given the profound impact of loneliness on the well-being of older adults, it's essential for healthcare providers, caregivers, and communities to implement strategies that encourage social interaction and emotional support for this vulnerable population.

Recognizing and empathizing with these emotional changes is essential for building a supportive and nurturing caregiving relationship. Your understanding and patience will play a pivotal role in assisting your aging parents through the emotional aspects of their journey.

The Challenges Along the Way

Now that you have insights into the physical, cognitive, and emotional changes your aging parents may experience, it's important to consider the challenges that come with your role as a caregiver. These challenges are an integral part of the caregiving journey and require thoughtful preparation for the sake of your parents' comfort, safety, and well-being.

Challenges Along the Caregiving Path

As you embark on this transformative caregiving journey for your aging parents, it's vital to recognize the multifaceted challenges that lie ahead. Each challenge presents an opportunity for growth and resilience, both for you and your loved ones. Let's explore deeper into these challenges to better understand how to navigate them effectively.

Challenge #1: Activities of Daily Living

Activities of Daily Living (ADLs), such as bathing, dressing, and meal preparation, can become increasingly challenging for the elderly due to age-related declines in physical and cognitive function. Factors like reduced muscle strength, decreased mobility, and diminished coordination contribute to difficulties in performing these essential tasks. Furthermore, chronic conditions like arthritis, vision impairment, or cognitive decline can exacerbate these challenges. Struggles with ADLs not only impact an individual's independence, but also significantly affect their quality of life and can lead to additional health problems. For instance, difficulty in preparing meals may result in poor nutrition, while challenges in personal hygiene can increase the risk of skin infections or other health issues. Addressing these challenges often involves a multidisciplinary approach, including physical therapy, occupational therapy, and support from caregivers, to help seniors maintain their independence and quality of life.

Challenge #2: Keeping Your Parents Safe

Keeping elderly parents safe presents a multifaceted challenge that encompasses both physical and emotional well-being. As they age, parents often face declining mobility, decreased strength, and a higher risk of chronic conditions, all of which make them more susceptible to accidents, particularly falls. Cognitive decline can also present safety risks, such as forgetfulness that leads to unattended stovetops or missed medications. Emotional vulnerabilities, like loneliness or depression, can further compound the challenge, making seniors more susceptible to scams or financial exploitation.

To address these issues, families often need to consider modifications to the home environment, regular medical check-ups, and possibly in-home care or assisted living arrangements. Monitoring systems and emergency response services can also offer an added layer of security. The goal is to balance safety considerations with the preservation of their independence and dignity, which often requires a delicate and tailored approach.

Challenge #3: Cost Concerns

Financial concerns are a significant challenge for many elderly individuals, particularly as healthcare costs continue to rise and the likelihood of needing prolonged medical or assisted care increases with age. Many seniors are on fixed incomes, such as pensions or Social Security, which may not adequately cover the escalating expenses associated with medications, regular medical check-ups, in-home care, or assisted living facilities. The cost of adapting a home for accessibility, purchasing mobility aids, or even the day-to-day costs of a healthy diet can strain limited resources.

These financial pressures not only affect the individual's quality of life but can also lead to choices that compromise health and safety, such as rationing medications or avoiding necessary medical treatments. Therefore, addressing cost concerns is a crucial aspect of holistic geriatric care and may involve exploring various financial assistance programs, insurance options, and low-cost healthcare services.

Challenge #4: Emergencies

Emergencies pose a unique and often heightened set of challenges in the elderly population due to their increased vulnerability to health issues, reduced mobility, and often slower response times. Whether it's a fall, a sudden illness, or a natural disaster, emergencies can have more severe consequences for an older adult than for a younger individual.

Many seniors live with chronic conditions that require ongoing medication or treatment, making it critical to maintain access to healthcare even in emergency situations. Cognitive decline or sensory impairments can further complicate responses to emergencies, impeding understanding or recognition of the situation and the steps needed for safety. Consequently, preparedness plans tailored to the needs of the elderly, such as easily accessible emergency kits with essential medications, or emergency response systems specifically designed for seniors, are vital for mitigating risks and ensuring rapid, appropriate care.

Challenge #5: Self-Care Concerns

Caregivers of the elderly often face significant challenges related to self-care, given the physical and emotional demands of caregiving. The constant attention required to manage an older adult's medical needs, mobility issues, and psychological well-being can lead caregivers to neglect their own health and self-care routines. This can result in caregiver burnout, characterized by symptoms of physical exhaustion, emotional fatigue, and even depression.

Studies show that caregivers are at increased risk for chronic conditions such as hypertension, diabetes, and heart disease due to elevated stress levels and lack of time for exercise or proper nutrition (Xu et al., 2019). Moreover, the emotional toll of caregiving can lead to strained family relationships and increased social isolation. Therefore, self-care for caregivers is not merely an option but a necessity, requiring support in the form of respite care, counseling, and medical check-ups to maintain their well-being and sustain their caregiving roles effectively.

By acknowledging and preparing for these challenges, you'll be better equipped to handle the caregiving journey ahead. It's a journey marked by selflessness, love, and dedication, where you play a pivotal role in enhancing the quality of life for your aging parents. Remember, support is available, and seeking help when needed is an act of wisdom and strength.

Embracing Your Role as a Caregiver

Now that you have a deeper understanding of the changes your aging parents may face, let's explore your pivotal role as their caregiver. Your responsibilities, expectations, and knowing when to seek professional assistance are all essential aspects of providing the best care for your loved ones.

The Caregiver's Role: A Multifaceted Journey

As a caregiver for your aging parents, your role is both diverse and indispensable. You become their primary source of support, responsible for their overall well-being, safety, and comfort. Here's an in-depth look at the key facets of your role as a caregiver:

- **Providing daily assistance:** Your foremost responsibility is assisting your aging parents with daily activities that may become challenging for them. Tasks like bathing, dressing, eating, and using the bathroom can gradually require your support, allowing them to maintain their independence for as long as possible.

- **Ensuring safety:** Creating a safe living environment for your parents is paramount. Identifying potential hazards and implementing preventive measures, especially if they have mobility issues, is essential to reduce the risk of accidents and falls.

- **Managing healthcare:** You play a pivotal role in managing your parents' healthcare needs. This involves keeping track of their medications, scheduling medical appointments, and facilitating communication with healthcare professionals to ensure they receive the necessary care and attention.

- **Emotional support:** Caregiving extends beyond physical tasks; it encompasses providing emotional support to your aging parents. Be prepared to lend a compassionate ear, offer companionship, and help them navigate the emotional challenges that may arise during this journey.

- **Household responsibilities:** In addition to caregiving tasks, you may need to assume household responsibilities that your parents can no longer manage. This could encompass tasks such as cooking, cleaning, grocery shopping, and other essential household chores.

- **Monitoring health:** Regularly monitoring your parents' health is imperative. Stay vigilant for any changes in their physical or cognitive condition and be prepared to take prompt action or seek medical attention when necessary.

- **Coordination and advocacy:** You may find yourself coordinating various aspects of your parents' care, including collaborating with other family members, managing financial matters, and advocating on their behalf within the complex healthcare system.

Knowing When to Seek Professional Help: Honoring Your Limits

While shouldering numerous responsibilities as a caregiver, it's essential to acknowledge your own limitations.

Recognizing and honoring your limits is crucial in various aspects of life, from caregiving roles to professional settings and personal relationships. When stress levels are consistently high, physical, and emotional fatigue sets in, or a sense of being overwhelmed persists, these are often signs that it's time to seek professional help. Ignoring these signals can lead to burnout, a reduced effectiveness in your role, and can also have detrimental effects on your health.

Whether it's talking to a medical doctor about persistent symptoms, seeking mental health counseling for ongoing emotional struggles, or consulting specialists for targeted advice in caregiving or job-related tasks, professional guidance can offer valuable insights and coping strategies. Don't hesitate to seek professional assistance or support from other family members. Enlisting the services of professional caregivers or healthcare providers ensures that your parents receive the best possible care while preserving your own well-being. This isn't an admission of failure; rather, it's a responsible step in maintaining your well-being and ensuring you're best equipped to handle the challenges you face.

By embracing your role as a caregiver and understanding both its challenges and rewards, you embark on a journey of compassion, resilience, and unwavering love. Your dedication will significantly enhance the quality of life for your aging parents while strengthening the bonds of your family. Remember, caregiving is a deeply personal journey, and it's important to use your best judgment. If you find certain responsibilities beyond your capacity, seek assistance to ensure that both you and your parents can navigate this journey.

With this foundational knowledge of what to expect from your aging parents and your role as a caregiver, you are better equipped to understand the various topics covered in this book. In the upcoming chapters, we will explore specific challenges, solutions, and strategies to provide the best care for your parents while maintaining their dignity and respect.

Chapter 2:

The Winds of Change: Transitions and Role Reversal

In life, change is an ever-present. However, few changes are as profound and challenging as those experienced when the roles we've always known are suddenly reversed. Chapter 2 helps you understand the various hearts of this transformation, exploring the concept of role reversal—a phenomenon that many adult children find themselves confronting as their aging parents require increasing care and support.

The Journey of a 35-Year-Old Woman

To embark on this exploration, let's first step into the shoes of a 35-year-old woman who found herself unprepared. She became the primary caregiver for her aging father, a man who had recently suffered two strokes, the second one being a fairly recent development. Although her mother was in better physical shape than her father, she, too, was aging, and certain physical tasks were beyond her capacity to handle alone.

Our protagonist willingly stepped into the role of caregiver, a journey that would test her love, resilience, and adaptability in profound ways. She became responsible for preparing her father's meals—which had to be carefully crafted to minimize the risk of choking—feeding him, managing his medications (while her mother had her own to attend to), bathing him, and assisting with his physical therapy exercises to help him regain some fine motor movement in his right arm, which had been affected by the stroke. In a humorous yet poignant moment, she referred to this experience as "parenting her parent"—a phrase that resonates with many who find themselves in similar circumstances.

This heartfelt story encapsulates the essence of role reversal, a journey that many adult children embark upon as they witness their parents' changing needs and capacities. But why is this phenomenon a matter of concern? Why should you, as a reader, seek to understand it and learn how to manage it?

Role Reversal: Unpacking the Significance

Role Reversal is a concept that extends far beyond a simple redistribution of caregiving duties; it represents a profound transformation that delves deep into the very essence of familial relationships. In this chapter, we embark on a journey of exploration, seeking to unravel the multifaceted dimensions and significance of role reversal as it pertains to caring for aging parents.

At its core, role reversal signifies a shift in the fundamental roles and dynamics that have been ingrained in our family structures for a lifetime. It challenges the traditional parent-child relationship we've known and brings into question the balance of power, responsibility, and interdependence within the family unit.

Throughout the course of this chapter, we will delve into the heart of role reversal, examining not only the practical implications but also the profound emotional and psychological impact it has on all parties involved. We will explore:

- **The essence of role reversal:** What does it mean when the roles we've known for a lifetime start to shift?

How does it impact our sense of self and our relationships with our parents? Examining the emotional landscape, we will dissect the intricate layers of role reversal, shedding light on the challenges and rewards that come with this transformation.

- **The evolution of caregiving:** As the torch of caregiving passes from one generation to another, we'll explore how this evolution shapes the dynamics within the family. What new responsibilities and obligations emerge, and how do they redefine our familial bonds? By examining the changing nature of caregiving, we can better understand the journey ahead.

- **Managing role reversal with empathy**: Recognizing that role reversal often brings emotional turmoil, we will discuss the importance of empathy and communication. How can we approach this transformation with grace and understanding, both for ourselves and our aging parents? Discovering the power of empathy, we can pave a path toward smoother transitions.

- **The role of acceptance:** Perhaps most significantly, we will explore the role of acceptance into the role of acceptance in embracing role reversal. What does it mean to accept these changes, and how can it lead to personal growth and strengthened familial bonds? By embracing the shifts with grace and adaptability, we can accomplish this transformative journey more effectively.

As we journey through these themes, we will shed light on role reversal, recognizing its significance not only in terms of caregiving responsibilities but also in its potential to shape and enrich our understanding of family, compassion, and the human experience.

The Challenges of Caregiving: The Multifaceted Terrain

Caregiving is a multifaceted journey, one marked by emotional, physical, and practical challenges that can significantly impact our lives. In caregiving, we find ourselves confronted by a myriad of questions and uncertainties, seeking to understand its influence on our daily existence, careers, and personal well-being.

- **Emotional challenges:** At the heart of caregiving lie emotional challenges that can be as demanding as they are profound. The emotional toll of witnessing our aging parents' struggles and vulnerability can weigh heavily on our hearts. We grapple with feelings of sadness, frustration, guilt, and helplessness, all while striving to provide the best care possible. How do we manage these complex emotions? How can we find strength in vulnerability and resilience in the face of adversity?

- **Physical challenges:** The physical demands of caregiving can be physically taxing, often requiring us to juggle multiple responsibilities. From assisting with daily tasks to managing healthcare needs, we may find ourselves stretched thin, affecting our own physical well-being. How can we strike a balance between caregiving and self-care? What strategies can help us maintain our vitality while fulfilling our caregiving duties?

- **Practical challenges:** Caregiving extends into the practical aspects of our lives, impacting our routines, careers, and daily responsibilities. Balancing caregiving with our personal and professional commitments can be a formidable challenge. How do we manage our careers while caring for our aging parents? What practical solutions can help us navigate this intricate juggling act?

The Power of Compassion: Illuminating the Path

In the midst of these challenges, compassion emerges as our guiding light, illuminating the path through role reversal. Compassion not only fuels the empathy needed to understand the aging parent's experience but also fosters resilience in the caregiver, helping them address difficulties with grace and fortitude. It creates a sense of mutual respect and dignity, making tasks such as physical care, medical treatment, and even difficult conversations more manageable and less fraught with tension.

Compassion can have a multiplier effect, inspiring others in the family or caregiving community to act similarly, thereby creating a nurturing environment conducive to the well-being of the elderly. At its core, compassion is more than just a virtue; it's an active choice that elevates the quality of care, enriches emotional bonds, and, ultimately, enhances the lives of both the caregiver and the recipient. It empowers us to cultivate patience, empathy, and resilience, offering solace in moments of frustration and strength in moments of vulnerability.

Cultivating Compassion

We explore the transformative potential of compassion and how it can shape our caregiving journey. What practices can help us develop a compassionate mindset? How can we learn to view caregiving as an act of love and devotion rather than a burden?

Cultivating compassion involves intentional practice and mindfulness, focusing on empathy and understanding toward oneself and others. It often starts with self-compassion, forgiving oneself for imperfections and understanding one's own emotional needs. This self-awareness then becomes the basis for extending compassion outward, encouraging a non-judgmental, empathetic approach to understanding the struggles and needs of other people.

Compassionate acts, whether big or small, not only benefit the recipients but also have a positive impact on the giver, often leading to increased feelings of happiness and a sense of purpose. Through daily practices like active listening, offering emotional support, and even simple acts of kindness, compassion can become a habitual response, enriching our lives and the lives of those around us.

Balancing the Relationship

The concept of "navigating the dance" in caregiving captures the intricate balance and fluidity required in the caregiver-care recipient relationship. The shifts are not always predetermined;

this means being attuned to the ever-changing physical and emotional needs of the care recipient, while also managing one's own well-being. There's an ebb and flow to the caregiver's role, sometimes leading, other times following, and often improvising. One moment may call for the firm guidance of a medical decision, while the next may require the gentle grace of emotional support.

Missteps are inevitable, whether they are misunderstandings or moments of fatigue. Skill, empathy, and patience, honed over time, make the journey smoother and more harmonious. Caregiving is most effective when compassion and understanding are the guiding forces.

The Importance of Preparedness: Equipping Ourselves for the Journey

To embark on this caregiving journey with confidence and resilience, preparedness becomes a cornerstone of our approach. It is crucial to understand why preparedness is essential and how it can mitigate the challenges and burdens caregiving can bring.

Preparedness is a cornerstone of effective caregiving for adult children looking after their aging parents. As parents age, their needs can change rapidly, making planning and preparation vital for managing a range of situations, from medical emergencies to the slower, yet equally challenging, progression of chronic conditions. Being prepared involves a host of activities such as researching healthcare options, understanding medical histories, and knowing the location of important documents like wills and medical directives. Financial planning is another crucial aspect, as caregiving can bring unexpected costs that affect the entire family.

Preparedness isn't solely about logistical or financial arrangements; it also encompasses emotional and psychological readiness. Understanding the emotional toll that caregiving can take helps in setting realistic expectations and seeking timely support. Educational resources and support networks, often available through community organizations and healthcare providers, can equip caregivers with the skills and resilience needed for this challenging role. Preparedness, in this context, becomes an ongoing process of gathering information, adapting to new circumstances, and seeking both professional and emotional support; thereby ensuring not just the well-being of the aging parent, but also the health and emotional stability of the caregiver.

Tools and Resources

A range of tools and resources is available to assist in this complex journey. Acquiring the knowledge and tools to advocate in healthcare can come from multiple avenues. Technology offers practical solutions, such as medical alert systems, medication reminders, and telehealth services, to help monitor health and safety remotely. Numerous websites and mobile apps provide comprehensive information on medical conditions, caregiving tips, and legal and financial planning.

On a more interpersonal level, support groups—both online and in-person—can offer emotional assistance and a sense of community, providing caregivers a platform to share experiences and learn from others in similar situations. Government agencies and nonprofit organizations often offer services like respite care, meal delivery, and transportation assistance, while geriatric care managers can provide personalized guidance on healthcare and long-term planning. Books and educational workshops focused on caregiving skills, stress management, and even specialized training for conditions like dementia or Parkinson's are other valuable resources.

Leveraging these tools can not only improve the quality of care for the aging parent but also significantly reduce the emotional and physical burden on the caregiver.

Embarking on the journey of caring for aging parents is a multifaceted experience that requires not just logistical preparation but also emotional fortitude. Uncovering insights, strategies, and perspectives becomes vital to equipping us with the resilience and compassion needed for this role. Research, education, and networking can provide invaluable information on best practices in caregiving, from managing chronic illnesses to understanding legal aspects of guardianship.

But, beyond the practical, immersing oneself in caregiver support groups or talking to experts can offer psychological coping mechanisms that enhance resilience. Personal stories and shared experiences can widen perspectives, teaching us how to handle complex emotions and situations. Books, webinars, or even meditative practices focused on mindfulness can cultivate compassion, a key ingredient that sustains us when challenges seem overwhelming. These resources collectively serve as a toolkit for emotional well-being, empowering us to be not just efficient caregivers but also empathetic individuals who can fully engage in the profound, transformative experience of caring for our aging parents.

"Parenting My Parent"

The concept of "parenting my parent" refers to the role reversal that often occurs when adult children become caregivers for their aging parents. This shift is emotionally complex and can be disorienting for both parties involved. Where once the parent provided guidance, structure, and support, now the adult child takes on these responsibilities, sometimes even managing aspects of daily living such as feeding, bathing, and healthcare decisions for their parents. The change can provoke a myriad of emotions, including sadness, frustration, and even resentment, as both parties grapple with issues of independence, dignity, and vulnerability.

For the adult child, the new caregiving role often comes with a steep learning curve that includes mastering medical jargon, legal paperwork, and perhaps even becoming a financial advisor for their parents. There can be psychological challenges too, such as setting boundaries and dealing with emotional stress, all while possibly juggling their own family, career, and personal needs. The parent, meanwhile, may struggle with a sense of loss or diminishment, feeling uncomfortable or even ashamed of needing to rely on their children for care.

- **Making life-changing decisions:** One of the most profound aspects of role reversal is the responsibility of making pivotal life decisions for our aging parents. In the past, they guided us through life's challenges, but now, the roles have shifted. From healthcare choices to financial matters, these decisions can weigh heavily on caregivers, who strive to make choices aligned with their parents' best interests.

- **Seeing our parents as vulnerable:** Witnessing our parents in a state of vulnerability, weakness, or dependence can be an emotionally charged experience. We may have never seen them in this light before, and it can be a stark reminder of the passage of time and the inevitability of aging. This transition can be both heart-wrenching and enlightening, as it deepens our understanding of our parents' humanity.

- **Being the voice of reason:** In moments of disagreement or conflict, caregivers often find themselves in the role of the mediator and voice of reason. This shift in dynamics can be challenging, as we must maintain respect and empathy through delicate discussions and disagreements while maintaining respect and empathy.

- **Responsibility for health and well-being:** Assuming responsibility for the health and well-being of another person, especially someone older than we, can be overwhelming. Caregivers must adapt to new routines, medications, and healthcare decisions, all while ensuring their parents' safety and comfort.

- **Caring for those who once cared for us:** Perhaps one of the most poignant aspects of role reversal is the act of caring for the individuals who once cared for us. This reversal of roles symbolizes the cyclical nature of life and the enduring love between parents and their children.

Despite its challenges, "parenting your parent" can also be a deeply rewarding experience, providing an opportunity for closeness, mutual understanding, and emotional growth for both parent and child. With open communication, empathy, and a bit of patience, this role reversal can serve as a poignant stage in the lifelong parent-child relationship.

Shifting Family Dynamics

As we continue to explore the of role reversal in the context of caring for aging parents, it becomes abundantly clear that comprehending and accepting the shifting family dynamics are fundamental prerequisites for success. These dynamics encompass a range of emotional, psychological, and practical changes that occur as adult children assume caregiving responsibilities for their aging parents.

The significance of this understanding goes beyond mere recognition; it extends to the vital aspect of learning how to manage these evolving dynamics adeptly. This management is not about resisting or attempting to revert to previous family roles but about finding a harmonious balance that accommodates the new responsibilities and relationships that arise during the caregiving process.

Ultimately, embracing these shifts with grace and adaptability will not only contribute to a smoother caregiving experience but also foster stronger bonds within the family. By acknowledging and addressing these changing dynamics head-on, you can forge a path that not only supports the well-being of your aging parent but also enriches your own personal growth and family connections.

Three Possible Parental Reactions to Role Reversal

- **Stubborn:** Some parents may resist the idea of role reversal and caregiving, often displaying stubbornness. This resistance can manifest as a reluctance to accept assistance, refusal to acknowledge their limitations, or a desire to maintain control over their lives.

- **Defensive:** Other parents may react defensively to role reversal, perceiving it as an intrusion into their independence. They may feel that their abilities are being questioned, leading to defensiveness and resistance to any changes in their routines or living arrangements.

- **Withdrawn:** For some parents, the emotional weight of role reversal can lead to withdrawal. They may become distant, experiencing a sense of vulnerability that makes them retreat from family interactions. This withdrawal can create challenges in communication and emotional connection.

Managing these varying reactions requires patience, empathy, and an understanding of the delicate balance between preserving the parent-child relationship and addressing the evolving caregiving responsibilities. "The key to managing this transition successfully is to know what part of your parent-child relationship has changed and to embrace it. And, to know which part of the relationship hasn't changed and to protect it" (Drake, 2021).

For caregivers, the experience of role reversal can be demanding, and its impact on family dynamics is profound. Several themes emerge when examining the repercussions of caregiving: changes in family relationships, shifting priorities, the toll of caregiving on mental and emotional well-being, and the significance of support systems.

Caregivers often find themselves in the position of making life-altering decisions for their aging parents, a role that can create tension and even resentment. The pressure of caregiving can be particularly intense when resources and coping mechanisms are lacking. It underscores the importance of fostering a support network and accessing available resources to alleviate the burdens that caregivers may face.

However, amidst the challenges, role reversal can also offer unique opportunities for growth and intimacy. Positive caregiving relationships can strengthen emotional bonds between parents and adult children, fostering an intimacy that may not have existed before. This journey of mutual care and support presents an opportunity for both parties to learn and grow, enriching their lives in ways that extend beyond physical care.

For aging parents, having their children actively involved in their care can significantly enhance their quality of life. The emotional connection that arises from this familial support can bring happiness and fulfillment. While it may not reverse aging-related health issues, it can certainly contribute to overall well-being.

Role reversal can be an emotionally turbulent journey, and it's crucial to recognize the gamut of feelings that may arise. Whether you experience a sense of unease, sadness, or any other emotion in response to the shifting dynamics within your family, understand that these sentiments are entirely normal. You are not alone in grappling with this transformation. Nonetheless, it's imperative to adopt constructive strategies to manage these emotions effectively, which will ultimately enable you to wholeheartedly embrace the caregiving journey for your aging parent.

Recent research, exemplified by the study published in Frontiers in Public Health (2019), has identified several themes that offer valuable insights into the emotional impact of role reversal:

- **Believing in the inherent value of family care:** Recognize and appreciate the significance and intrinsic value of providing care within the family. Understand that the bonds and connections formed during caregiving can be immensely rewarding, enriching both your life and your parent's.

- **Making sense of the changing nature of caregiving:** Acknowledge that caregiving roles are subject to evolution, and these changes are a natural part of the life cycle. Embracing the fluidity of these dynamics can help you adapt more effectively to the evolving needs of your aging parent.

- **"Making the best of it":** Cultivate a positive outlook on your caregiving role. Instead of dwelling on the challenges, focus on the opportunities for growth and connection that it presents. By embracing this perspective, you can transform your role into a source of personal fulfillment and shared joy with your parents.

These themes serve as guiding principles in role reversal, helping you to find meaning and purpose in this journey. Building upon these three central themes of motivation and drawing from the insights provided by the sources mentioned earlier, let's explore five effective strategies that can help you cope with the transitions and emotional impact of role reversal when caring for your aging parents. These strategies will provide valuable guidance as you navigate this journey.

Allow Yourself to "Mourn" the Loss of Traditional Roles

Caring for aging parents often means a significant shift in family dynamics. The roles you've known your entire life may suddenly change. It's entirely normal to feel a sense of loss for the roles that once defined your relationship with your parents. This can manifest as grief or sadness. By acknowledging these feelings and allowing yourself to "mourn" the traditional roles, you validate your emotions. Remember that this process is part of adjusting to the new reality and doesn't diminish the love and care you have for your parents.

Prioritize Open Communication, Always

Effective communication is a cornerstone of successful caregiving. Try to maintain open and honest conversations with your aging parents. Share your feelings, concerns, and thoughts about the evolving family dynamics. Encourage your parents to do the same. Transparency fosters trust and understanding, helping you resolve challenges together. These conversations can also provide insight into your parents' wishes and preferences, making it easier to provide the care and support they need.

Realize Your Parents are Also Struggling

While role reversal can be challenging for adult children, it's important to recognize that your aging parents are navigating their own difficulties. They may grapple with feelings of vulnerability, dependence, or the loss of autonomy. Demonstrating empathy and understanding can create a supportive environment where your parents feel heard and respected. By acknowledging their challenges, you can work together to find solutions that enhance their well-being.

Maintain Respect for Your Parents

Regardless of role reversal, your parents remain deserving of the same respect and dignity you've always shown them. It's crucial to remember that while their needs may have changed, their identity as your parents has not. Treating them with respect not only upholds their sense of self-worth but also preserves the love and trust that form the foundation of your relationship. Approach caregiving with the same reverence you've had for your parents, and you'll nurture a sense of mutual respect.

Maintain Boundaries and Be Firm About Them

Healthy boundaries are essential for both caregivers and their aging parents. Clearly define the limits of what you can and cannot do, considering your own well-being and capacity. Encourage your parents to establish their boundaries as well. Boundaries not only protect your physical and emotional health but also promote a sense of autonomy for your parents. This balance will be discussed in greater detail in a later chapter, offering practical strategies for maintaining these essential boundaries.

Chapter 3:

Parents' Physical and Mental State: Health and Wellbeing

In this chapter, we will examine both physical and mental health concerning the aging process. We will explore various health issues that caregivers should be well-informed about, equipping them with the knowledge to effectively address and manage these concerns, encompassing chronic conditions as well as mental health challenges.

Advocating for Your Parents' Needs: A Lesson in Compassion

In a small house, nestled amidst a peaceful neighborhood, lived the Parker family. The heart of the home was their beloved mother, Margaret, a woman of grace and resilience who had been battling stage 4 cancer. Her days had become a courageous fight against the relentless disease, leaving her bed-bound and weakened.

One fateful day, Margaret's health took another challenging turn. She was admitted to the hospital due to a severe bout of pneumonia. The family, already well-acquainted with the harsh realities of cancer, had been through numerous trials together, but this new development brought fresh concerns and decisions to the forefront.

The hospital room became a temporary refuge, where Margaret was connected to an oxygen mask, a feeding tube, and an IV drip. Despite the medical intervention, her breathing remained labored and strained. The medical team presented a proposal— a delicate yet invasive procedure involving an incision at her neck, allowing the insertion of a breathing tube. They explained the necessity of this intervention for her survival.

The family gathered around, their faces etched with worry and contemplation. They listened intently to the doctors, who cautiously conveyed the potential risks and complications. The proposed procedure came with the foreboding reality that the incision could become an open wound vulnerable to infection. Additionally, Margaret would have to endure another week of hospitalization, where she had already grown weary and tense.

As they stood by her bedside, the family exchanged glances and shared unspoken sentiments. They knew Margaret's feelings well, as she had already expressed her discomfort with the oxygen mask and other medical interventions. The room was filled not only with the hum of machines, but with the palpable love and connection that had bonded this family through countless trials.

In that solemn moment, the family reached a unanimous decision—a decision rooted in their deep love and understanding of Margaret. They chose to forego the proposed procedure, knowing that the discomfort and suffering it might bring would outweigh any potential benefits.

With courage in their hearts, they approached Margaret and gently shared their choice with her. Her eyes, weakened by illness yet still full of love, met theirs, and she nodded in agreement. The family understood that her comfort and peace were paramount.

They returned home, Margaret nestled in her bed, surrounded by the warm embrace of her family. Though she never fully recovered, her disposition greatly improved in the familiar and comforting surroundings of her home. Her final days were marked not by the sterile walls of a hospital room but by the love, care, and tenderness of her devoted family.

In their shared decision, they found solace, knowing that they had honored Margaret's wishes and provided her with the greatest gift of all—a peaceful and loving farewell in the sanctuary of her home, where family bonds remained unbroken.

The Healthcare System: Empowering Caregivers

To provide the best possible care for their aging parents while managing potential budget constraints, caregivers must manage the complex healthcare system effectively. This knowledge improves care coordination, informed cost-effective decision-making, and access to resources, ensures their parents receive optimal care tailored to their unique needs even when parents are still capable of rational thought and reasoning.

Tips for Effective Healthcare Management

- **Bring medications:** When accompanying your aging parents to medical appointments, always bring their medications with you. It's critical that healthcare workers have a list of current medications, strengths, and dosing.

- **Politeness matters:** Building positive relationships with healthcare professionals, especially nurses, can lead to better care for your parents. Being friendly, polite, and appreciative of their efforts can go a long way in ensuring quality treatment.

- **Review health insurance:** Take the time to review your parents' health insurance, ensuring it complies with the Affordable Care Act (ACA). Avoid the pitfalls of non-compliant plans, which may lead to unexpected and exorbitant costs.

- **Preemptive paperwork:** Prior to hospital visits or procedures, fill out paperwork in advance whenever possible. This reduces stress and streamlines the check-in process, ensuring a smoother experience for both caregivers and their parents.

- **Medicare awareness:** If your parent is covered by Medicare, be aware of the time limits and restrictions associated with the program. Understanding the Dintricacies of Medicare can help you make timely decisions about their healthcare.

Directing the healthcare system is not only about managing medical needs but also about safeguarding your parents' financial and emotional well-being. These tips empower caregivers to advocate effectively for their aging parents, ensuring they receive the best possible care within their budget and under the compassionate guidance of their loved ones.

Physical Health Management 101

Taking care of your parents' physical health as they age is an essential responsibility, even if you lack medical training or certification. In this section, we will examine common physical health challenges that elderly adults often face and equip you with the knowledge needed to monitor and address these issues effectively. Remember, you don't need to be a medical expert; you simply need to know how to recognize signs, when to seek professional help, and how to provide support.

Understanding Fatigue and Physical Weakness

What Is Fatigue?

Fatigue in the elderly is a common issue that can have various causes and impacts on their physical and mental well-being. Fatigue is not just a normal part of aging; it can be a symptom of underlying medical conditions or lifestyle factors. Understanding and addressing fatigue in the elderly is essential for maintaining their quality of life. Here's a closer look at fatigue in the elderly:

Causes of Fatigue

- **Medical Conditions:** Chronic medical conditions such as heart disease, diabetes, anemia, thyroid disorders, chronic obstructive pulmonary disease (COPD), and kidney disease can contribute to fatigue.

- **Medications:** Some medications commonly prescribed to older adults may cause fatigue as a side effect. These can include certain blood pressure medications, antihistamines, sedatives, and muscle relaxants.

- **Sleep Disorders:** Sleep problems, including insomnia, sleep apnea, and restless leg syndrome, can lead to poor sleep quality and daytime fatigue.

- **Dehydration:** Elderly individuals may be at a higher risk of dehydration, which can result in fatigue.

- **Nutritional deficiencies:** Deficiencies in essential nutrients like vitamin D, vitamin B12, and iron can lead to fatigue.

- **Depression and anxiety:** Mental health conditions, such as depression and anxiety, can cause fatigue as a symptom.

- **Pain:** Chronic pain conditions, such as arthritis or neuropathy, can interfere with sleep and lead to fatigue.

- **Infections:** Undiagnosed or untreated infections can result in fatigue.

- **Stress:** Chronic stress, including caregiving responsibilities, can contribute to fatigue.

- **Lack of physical activity:** A sedentary lifestyle can lead to muscle weakness and decreased energy levels.

Impact of Fatigue

- **Reduced quality of life:** Fatigue can limit an elderly person's ability to engage in social, recreational, and physical activities, leading to a diminished quality of life.

- **Increased fall risk:** Fatigue can lead to muscle weakness and impaired balance, increasing the risk of falls and injuries.

- **Cognitive impairment:** Chronic fatigue may affect cognitive function, including memory and concentration.

- **Mood changes:** Fatigue can contribute to irritability, mood swings, and feelings of frustration or helplessness.

Managing Fatigue

Managing fatigue in the elderly involves a multifaceted approach that addresses its underlying causes and promotes overall well-being. Fatigue can significantly impact an older adult's quality of life, so it's essential to identify the specific factors contributing to fatigue and implement strategies to alleviate it.

Here are some key steps in managing fatigue in the elderly:

- **Medical evaluation:** Start with a comprehensive medical assessment by a healthcare provider to identify any underlying medical conditions that may be causing or contributing to fatigue. This may involve blood tests, imaging, and other diagnostic measures.

- **Medication review:** Review the elderly person's medication regimen with their healthcare provider. Some medications can cause fatigue as a side effect, and adjustments or changes in medications may be necessary.

- **Address nutritional deficiencies:** Ensure that the elderly individual is receiving proper nutrition. Address any nutritional deficiencies, such as vitamin D, vitamin B12, iron, or folic acid, through dietary changes or supplements as recommended by a healthcare provider.

- **Manage chronic health conditions:** If the elderly person has chronic medical conditions like diabetes, heart disease, or thyroid disorders, ensure that these conditions are well-managed to reduce the impact of fatigue.

- **Sleep assessment:** Evaluate the individual's sleep patterns and quality of sleep. Address sleep disorders such as insomnia, sleep apnea, or restless leg syndrome through appropriate treatments, including lifestyle changes, medications, or medical devices.

- **Encourage physical activity:** Promote regular physical activity that is appropriate for the elderly person's fitness level. Exercise can improve muscle strength, balance, and overall energy levels.

- **Manage pain:** If the individual experiences chronic pain due to conditions like arthritis, neuropathy, or musculoskeletal issues, work with healthcare providers to develop a pain management plan that can improve comfort and reduce fatigue.

- **Stress management:** Teach stress management techniques such as relaxation exercises, mindfulness, or meditation to help reduce the emotional and physical impact of stress.

- **Maintain hydration:** Ensure that the elderly person is adequately hydrated, as dehydration can contribute to fatigue. Encourage regular fluid intake, especially in hot or dry climates.

- **Balanced diet:** Encourage a balanced diet that includes a variety of nutrients from fruits, vegetables, lean proteins, whole grains, and dairy products. Proper nutrition can help maintain energy levels.

- **Manage mental health:** Address any underlying mental health conditions such as depression or anxiety through therapy, counseling, or medication as recommended by a mental health professional.

- **Monitor medications:** Ensure that the elderly person takes their medications as prescribed and follows up with healthcare providers for medication adjustments or changes if needed.

- **Regular check-ups:** Schedule regular check-ups with healthcare providers to monitor and manage any ongoing health issues.

Social Engagement

- **Identify interests:** Ask parents to find out their interests, hobbies, and activities they enjoy. This could range from arts and crafts to gardening, book clubs, music, exercise, or cooking.

- **Form clubs or groups:** Based on the identified interests, create small clubs or groups. For example, if a group of seniors loves gardening, establish a gardening club. If they enjoy reading, start a book club.

- **Regular gatherings:** Plan regular gatherings for the clubs or groups. This could be weekly or monthly, depending on the preferences of the participants. These gatherings provide a consistent opportunity for social interaction.

- **Diverse activities:** Ensure that the activities cater to a variety of interests. This could include group discussions, hands-on workshops, outings to local places of interest, or virtual sessions.

- **Intergenerational activities:** Organize events that involve interactions with younger generations, such as visits from school students, where seniors can share their experiences and skills.

- **Tech assistance:** If the group is comfortable with technology, consider virtual meetings or activities using video conferencing platforms to connect with those who might not be able to attend in person.

- **Celebrate milestones:** Celebrate birthdays, holidays, and personal achievements within the group. This creates a sense of community and belonging.

- **Volunteer opportunities:** Engage the group in volunteer activities that align with their interests. This provides a sense of purpose and social engagement while giving back to the community.

- **Guest speakers:** Invite guest speakers to share on topics of interest, sparking discussions and enhancing the learning experience.

- **Support and friendship:** Foster an environment where members can openly share their thoughts, feelings, and experiences, providing a support network for one another.

- **Flexibility:** Be flexible in adapting activities to the needs and abilities of the group members. This ensures that everyone feels included and valued.

Balance Rest and Activity

Help the elderly person strike a balance between rest and activity. Adequate rest is essential for managing fatigue, but too much inactivity can contribute to muscle weakness and increased fatigue.

Educate Caregivers

If you are a caregiver, educate yourself about the specific needs and challenges of the elderly person you are caring for to provide appropriate support. It's important to tailor the management of fatigue to the individual's unique circumstances and needs. Working closely with healthcare providers and addressing the underlying causes of fatigue can help improve the elderly person's energy levels, overall health, and quality of life.

When Is Fatigue a Cause for Concern?

Fatigue in the elderly can be a common occurrence, but there are situations when it may be a cause for concern and require medical attention. Here are some guidelines to help determine when fatigue in the elderly should be considered a cause for concern:

- **Persistent and unexplained fatigue:** If an elderly individual experiences fatigue that persists for an extended period, such as several weeks or months, and there is no apparent reason for it (such as strenuous physical activity or lack of sleep), it may warrant investigation.

- **Sudden and severe fatigue:** If an elderly person suddenly experiences severe fatigue that is significantly different from their usual energy levels, it could be a sign of an underlying medical condition.

- **Accompanied by other symptoms:** Fatigue that is accompanied by other concerning symptoms, such as unexplained weight loss, fever, pain, shortness of breath, dizziness, or changes in bowel or urinary habits, should be evaluated by a healthcare professional.

- **Exacerbated by physical activity:** If fatigue is exacerbated by even minimal physical activity or exertion, it may indicate an issue with the heart, lungs, or circulatory system.

- **Mental changes:** Fatigue that is accompanied by changes in mental function, such as confusion, memory problems, or difficulty concentrating, may be indicative of an underlying medical condition, including infections or neurological disorders.

- **Previous medical conditions:** Individuals with preexisting medical conditions, such as heart disease, diabetes, anemia, or chronic kidney disease, may experience fatigue as a symptom of disease progression or medication side effects. In such cases, any changes in fatigue levels should be discussed with a healthcare provider.

- **Medication-related fatigue:** Certain medications commonly prescribed to the elderly can cause fatigue as a side effect. If an elderly person is taking multiple medications and experiences significant fatigue, it's important to consult with their healthcare provider to assess whether medication adjustments are necessary.

- **Falls or balance issues:** Fatigue can contribute to an increased risk of falls and balance problems in the elderly. If an older adult experiences fatigue that leads to a higher risk of falls, it should be addressed promptly to prevent injuries.

- **Worsening overall health:** If fatigue coincides with an overall decline in an elderly person's health, including reduced appetite, loss of interest in activities, or declining mobility, it may be a sign of a more significant health issue that needs evaluation.

In any of these situations, it is advisable for the elderly individual or their caregivers to seek medical advice from a healthcare professional. Fatigue can be a symptom of various medical conditions, ranging from anemia and infections to chronic diseases and cardiac issues. Early identification and management of the underlying cause can significantly improve an individual's well-being and quality of life.

Balance and Mobility Issues in Older Adults

As we age, our balance and mobility can undergo significant changes, affecting our daily lives and increasing the risk of accidents. Understanding the reasons behind these changes and how to address them is crucial for supporting your aging parents' overall well-being. In this section, we will explore why balance and mobility decline with age and provide actionable steps to help your parents improve and maintain their physical stability.

Why Does Balance and Mobility Decline With Age?

Balance tends to worsen with aging due to a combination of factors, including physiological changes in the body, decreased sensory input, changes in muscle mass and strength, and the increased risk of medical conditions and medications that can affect balance.

Here are some of the key reasons why balance tends to decline with aging:

- **Muscle weakness:** As people age, there is a natural decline in muscle mass and strength, a condition known as sarcopenia. Weak muscles, especially in the lower limbs, can make it more challenging to maintain balance and stability.

- **Joint stiffness:** Age-related changes in joints, including reduced flexibility and increased stiffness, can affect the range of motion and make it harder to adjust and maintain balance.

- **Sensory changes:** The sensory systems that contribute to balance, such as vision, proprioception (the sense of body position) and the vestibular system (inner ear balance), may experience age-related changes. For example, vision may deteriorate, making it harder to perceive environmental cues, and inner ear function can decline.

- **Decreased reflexes:** Reflexes that help maintain balance and respond to sudden changes in position may slow down with age, reducing the ability to recover from slips or trips.

- **Medications:** Older adults often take multiple medications, some of which can have side effects that affect balance, coordination, or cognitive function. Medications that cause dizziness or drowsiness can increase the risk of falls.

- **Chronic medical conditions:** Certain chronic health conditions, such as diabetes, peripheral neuropathy, arthritis, and cardiovascular disease, can affect balance and increase the risk of falls.

- **Reduced physical activity:** A sedentary lifestyle or reduced physical activity can contribute to muscle weakness, reduced flexibility, and a decline in overall fitness, all of which can impact balance.

- **Neurological changes:** Age-related changes in the central nervous system can affect the brain's ability to process sensory information and respond to balance challenges.

- **Cognitive changes:** Cognitive decline, which can occur with aging, can affect the ability to concentrate and make quick decisions, making it more difficult to respond to balance threats effectively.

- **Environmental factors:** Environmental hazards, such as uneven surfaces, poor lighting, and clutter, can pose a greater risk to older adults with declining balance.

It's important to note that while some decline in balance is a normal part of aging, it is not inevitable, and there are steps individuals can take to mitigate the effects. Regular physical activity, strength training exercises, balance training, and maintaining a healthy lifestyle can help improve or maintain balance in older adults. Additionally, addressing underlying medical conditions and regularly reviewing medications with healthcare providers can reduce the risk of balance-related issues and falls.

Despite precautions, emergencies such as falls, sprains, or broken bones can occur. Knowing how to respond swiftly and appropriately is crucial. By understanding the reasons behind age-related balance and mobility decline and implementing exercises and strategies to mitigate these issues, you can empower your parents to lead more active and independent lives. Additionally, knowing how to respond to emergency situations ensures their safety and well-being in challenging times.

Understanding and Strengthening Immunity in Aging Parents

As our loved one's journey through the golden years, understanding their aging bodies becomes paramount. One of the critical aspects that caregivers and family members should be well-versed in is the aging immune system. In this section, we explore why the immune system weakens with age, the dangers associated with a weakened immunity system, and proactive steps to bolster the immune defenses of aging parents.

The Aging Immune System: Why Does It Weaken?

Aging is a natural process, and so is the gradual decline of the immune system. Our immune system, once a vigilant defender, tends to become less efficient over the years. Researchers have been delving into this phenomenon to unlock its mysteries. Some of the reasons behind the weakening of the immune system in the elderly include:

- **Immunosenescence:** This term describes the natural aging of the immune system. It results in a decline in the production and function of immune cells and antibodies, making the body less responsive to pathogens.

- **Changes in immune cells:** Aging leads to changes in the composition and function of immune cells. T cells, for example, may become less effective at recognizing and attacking invaders.

- **Chronic Conditions:** The presence of chronic illnesses or diseases can further compromise the immune system, as the body is engaged in a constant battle against these conditions.

The Perils of Weakened Immunity

A weakened immune system poses significant dangers to aging parents. It leaves them vulnerable to various health threats, including infections, chronic illnesses, and more. The consequences of a weakened immunity system may include:

- **Increased infection risk:** Aging parents are more susceptible to infections like the flu, pneumonia, and urinary tract infections due to a less robust immune response.

- **Delayed recovery:** The weakened immune system may result in slower recovery times from illnesses and surgeries.

- **Chronic diseases:** Conditions such as cancer and autoimmune disorders may emerge or worsen due to immune dysregulation.

- **Effectiveness:** Vaccinations may be less effective in the elderly, reducing their protection against preventable diseases.

Strengthening Your Parents' Immune System

Empowering caregivers and family members to take proactive steps in supporting their aging parents' immune health is essential. There are various strategies that can help strengthen the immune system, including:

- **Nutrition:** Ensure a balanced diet rich in vitamins, minerals, and antioxidants. Consider dietary supplements if needed.

- **Exercise:** Encourage regular physical activity, even if it's gentle exercises like walking or yoga, to boost overall health.

- **Stress management:** Chronic stress can weaken the immune system. Teach stress-reduction techniques such as meditation and deep breathing.

- **Adequate sleep:** Ensure aging parents get sufficient and restful sleep, as sleep is crucial for immune function.

- **Vaccinations:** Stay current with recommended vaccines, which can provide essential protection against specific diseases.

Recognizing Signs of Immunological Problems

Vigilance is key when it comes to monitoring the health of aging parents. Knowing the signs that may indicate immunological issues and how to respond is crucial. Look out for signs like persistent fever, unexplained weight loss, chronic fatigue, or frequent infections. If such symptoms arise, prompt consultation with healthcare professionals is imperative. In cases of emergency, it's vital to be aware of the warning signs that may require immediate attention, such as severe respiratory distress or high fever.

Understanding the aging immune system, its vulnerabilities, and the methods to fortify it is essential for ensuring the health and well-being of aging parents. Armed with knowledge and proactive measures, caregivers and family members can play a pivotal role in supporting their loved ones as they navigate the challenges of immune health in their later years.

Caring for Bed-Bound Patients: Ensuring Comfort and Health

Many older adults, particularly those with chronic illnesses or diseases, may find themselves bed-bound during their later years. Providing care for bed-bound patients requires specific knowledge and a commitment to their well-being and comfort. In this section, we will explore the responsibilities of caregivers and crucial considerations, with a particular focus on preventing and managing bedsores, which are a significant health risk for bed-bound individuals.

It is imperative to mention that if your loved one will be bed-bound for more than a day or two, you can request your provider to order a home health aide.

Home health aides are trained professionals who provide essential in-home care and assistance to individuals who need help with activities of daily living (ADLs) and basic healthcare tasks. They play a crucial role in supporting individuals, particularly those who are elderly, disabled, or recovering from illness or surgery, to maintain their independence and stay in the comfort of their own homes. Here are some key aspects of home health aides and their role:

- **Personal care:** Home health aides assist with personal hygiene tasks, including bathing, grooming, dressing, and toileting.

- **Mobility assistance:** They help clients with mobility and transfers, which may involve using mobility aids or assisting individuals in moving from bed to chair, for example.

- **Medication reminders:** Home health aides can remind clients to take their medications as prescribed, although they do not typically administer medications.

- **Meal preparation:** They prepare meals and ensure that clients receive proper nutrition according to dietary restrictions or preferences.

- **Light housekeeping:** Aides may perform light housekeeping tasks such as cleaning, laundry, and tidying up to maintain a safe and comfortable living environment.

- **Companionship:** Providing companionship and emotional support is an essential aspect of their role, helping to reduce feelings of isolation and loneliness.

- **Transportation:** Some home health aides can assist with transportation to medical appointments, grocery shopping, or other errands.

- **Monitoring health:** They may help monitor vital signs, report changes in the client's condition to healthcare professionals, and assist with exercises or rehabilitation routines.

- **Safety checks:** Home health aides assess the home environment for safety hazards and implement measures to prevent accidents or falls.

Personal care services will most likely be covered by health insurance, Medicare, Medicaid, or long-term care insurance, depending on eligibility and specific circumstances.

Responsibilities in Caring for Bed-Bound Patients

Caring for bed-bound patients is a multifaceted task that encompasses several critical responsibilities. Caregivers should be aware of the following considerations:

- **Hygiene and comfort:** Regularly attend to the patient's hygiene needs, including changing bedding, cleaning, and ensuring they are comfortable. Proper positioning is essential to prevent pressure ulcers.

- **Nutrition and hydration:** Ensure that the patient receives adequate nutrition and hydration, as a balanced diet and sufficient fluids are vital for overall health and recovery.

- **Mobility and exercise:** Implement gentle range-of-motion exercises to prevent muscle atrophy and joint stiffness. Reposition the patient regularly to avoid pressure on specific areas.

- **Medication management:** Administer medications as prescribed by healthcare professionals and monitor their effects.

- **Communication:** Maintain open and compassionate communication with the patient, addressing their emotional needs and providing companionship.

- **Monitoring health:** Keep a close eye on the patient's vital signs, any signs of discomfort or pain, and report any concerning changes to healthcare providers.

- **Bedsores prevention:** Take proactive steps to prevent bedsores, which can be life-threatening for bed-bound patients.

Bedsores: Risks and Prevention

Bedsores, also known as pressure ulcers, are a significant concern for bed-bound patients. These painful skin lesions result from prolonged pressure on the skin and underlying tissue. They can lead to serious complications, such as infections and tissue damage. It's crucial to understand the risks and preventive measures:

- **Risks:** Bedsores are more likely to develop in areas where the bones are close to the skin's surface, such as the heels, hips, tailbone, and elbows. Factors like immobility, poor nutrition, moisture, and friction increase the risk.

- **Prevention:** To prevent bedsores, caregivers should frequently reposition the patient, provide a supportive mattress or cushion, keep the skin clean and dry, and ensure proper nutrition. Regularly inspect the skin for any signs of pressure sores, such as redness, warmth, or skin breakdown.

Caring for bed-bound patients requires diligence, compassion, and a comprehensive understanding of their specific needs. Prioritizing hygiene, nutrition, mobility, and proactive prevention of bedsores are essential elements of providing quality care to these vulnerable individuals. It's crucial to be vigilant in preventing and managing bedsores, as they can have severe consequences for the health and well-being of elderly bed-bound patients.

Cognitive Conditions and Concerns in Aging

Understanding cognitive changes associated with aging is a critical aspect of providing comprehensive care for older adults. While some cognitive changes are considered typical with age, it's essential to recognize when these changes may warrant attention from a healthcare professional. In this section, we will explore cognitive issues commonly associated with healthy aging, drawing comparisons to those that may signal more serious concerns.

Normal Cognitive Changes vs. Red Flags

As we discussed in Chapter 1, cognitive changes are a natural part of aging. It's important to revisit the "Cognitive Changes" list to differentiate typical age-related changes from those that may indicate more serious conditions such as dementia or mild cognitive impairment.

It's essential to emphasize that while dementia and mild cognitive impairment are common cognitive conditions, not all cognitive changes in older adults signify these conditions. As noted in the academic source, the phenotype of normal cognitive aging is well described, and some mental capabilities remain well maintained into old age (Zamorano & Quezada, 2021).

Factors Influencing Cognitive Aging

Understanding cognitive aging is complex, as various factors contribute to individual differences. Genetics, general health, and medical disorders like atherosclerotic disease, as well as biological processes like inflammation, neurobiological changes, diet, and lifestyle, all play a role in cognitive aging. It's worth noting that the effect sizes of these factors are often small, and some may be poorly replicated. In some instances, there is the possibility of reverse causation, where prior cognitive ability affects the factors believed to influence cognitive aging.

The Gradual Nature of Cognitive Aging

It's important to stress that cognitive decline during aging is typically gradual and not usually drastic or extreme. While exceptions are possible, they are uncommon. Most older adults experience some degree of cognitive change, but these changes often do not significantly impair their daily functioning.

Understanding the continuum of cognitive aging, from typical changes to more concerning signs, is crucial for caregivers and healthcare professionals alike. Recognizing when cognitive issues may require professional evaluation ensures that older adults receive appropriate care and support while enjoying the many facets of a fulfilling and active aging journey.

Understanding Dementia: Not a Normal Part of Aging

Dementia is a topic that warrants our attention, particularly in the context of aging parents. Contrary to popular belief, it is not a normal part of the aging process. While age can bring about changes in memory and cognitive function, dementia represents an extreme departure from what is considered typical. In this section, we will delve into what dementia looks like in aging patients and outline concerning symptoms that should prompt a healthcare check-up.

Dementia: An Aberration in Aging

Dementia is a broad term encompassing a range of cognitive impairments, with Alzheimer's disease being one of the most well-known forms. It is important to understand that dementia is not a typical outcome of aging; instead, it is a complex medical condition that affects memory, thinking, and behavior.

While it is true that memory may decline to some extent as we age, dementia takes this to an entirely different level. It can manifest in various ways, such as:

- **Memory loss:** Dementia often leads to profound and persistent memory loss, affecting the ability to recall recent events, names, and familiar faces.

- **Confusion with time and sequence:** People with dementia might lose track of time, struggle to differentiate between days, and have difficulty organizing events in chronological order.

- **Misplacing items:** Individuals with dementia often misplace items, sometimes putting them in unusual or illogical places. They might not remember where they put their keys, glasses, or other belongings.

- **Difficulty with daily tasks:** Everyday tasks like dressing, eating, and bathing may become challenging for those with dementia.

- **Personality changes:** Behavioral changes, mood swings, and alterations in personality are common symptoms.

- **Word recall and communication:** Dementia can affect the ability to find and use the right words, leading to difficulty in expressing thoughts and engaging in conversations. This can result in frustration and communication breakdowns.

- **False memories and confabulation:** As dementia progresses, some individuals might create false memories or confabulate (fabricate) stories to fill in gaps in their memory. They might genuinely believe these stories.

- **Difficulty learning new information:** Learning and retaining new information become challenging. Even if the person can remember something for a short period, it might be quickly forgotten. This makes it hard for them to acquire and integrate new knowledge or skills.

- **Long-term memory:** While long-term memories are often retained for a longer period, dementia can eventually affect these memories as well. The person might have difficulty recalling significant life events, names of family members, or places from their past.

- **Spatial memory issues:** Dementia can impact spatial memory, making it challenging to recognize locations or walk through familiar places. This can lead to getting lost even in familiar surroundings.

- **Prospective memory:** This refers to remembering to perform a task in the future. Individuals with dementia might forget appointments, events, or tasks they planned to do, causing disruptions in their daily routines.

- **Emotional impact:** Memory loss can lead to frustration, anxiety, and even depression as individuals realize they are struggling to remember things that were once easy for them.

Recognizing Warning Signs

Given the profound impact of dementia on individuals and their families, it is crucial to be vigilant about recognizing warning signs. Early intervention can greatly improve the quality of life for those affected. Here are some concerning symptoms that should prompt a healthcare check-up:

- **Memory loss:** Frequent and persistent memory lapses that disrupt daily life.

- **Difficulty with familiar tasks:** Struggling to perform tasks that were once routine, such as cooking or managing finances.

- **Confusion about time and place:** Getting disoriented or lost in familiar surroundings.

- **Poor judgment:** Making unusual or risky decisions that are out of character.

- **Changes in mood or personality:** Noticeable and unexplained mood swings, irritability, or personality changes.

Alzheimer's Disease

Alzheimer's disease is a progressive and irreversible neurological disorder that primarily affects memory, thinking, and behavior. It is the most common cause of dementia, accounting for approximately 60-80% of dementia cases (Alzheimer's Association, 2023). Alzheimer's disease gradually worsens over time, impacting an individual's ability to perform daily tasks and eventually leading to a loss of independence. Here are some key points to understand about Alzheimer's disease:

The Symptoms

Alzheimer's disease typically begins with subtle memory problems that gradually worsen. Common early symptoms include forgetting recent events or conversations, misplacing belongings, and difficulty solving familiar problems.

Later Symptoms

- **Memory loss:** Alzheimer's often involves severe memory loss, including the inability to remember recently learned information.

- **Difficulty with routine tasks:** Patients may struggle with daily tasks like dressing, grooming, and cooking.

- **Language problems:** Finding it challenging to follow or join in conversations and using incorrect words or phrases.

- **Disorientation:** Getting lost in familiar places or losing track of time.

- **Changes in mood and personality:** Becoming increasingly confused, suspicious, or anxious.

- **Brain changes:** Alzheimer's is characterized by abnormal protein deposits in the brain, including beta-amyloid plaques and tau tangles. These deposits interfere with communication between brain cells and ultimately lead to cell damage and cell death. Over time, this brain damage results in cognitive decline and memory loss.

Stages

Alzheimer's disease is often categorized into three stages: mild, moderate, and severe. In the mild stage, individuals may have memory lapses and difficulty with complex tasks. In the moderate stage, cognitive decline becomes more pronounced, and individuals may require assistance with daily activities. In the severe stage, individuals lose the ability to communicate and care for themselves.

Risk Factors

Age is the most significant risk factor for Alzheimer's disease, with the risk increasing significantly after the age of 65. Other risk factors include genetics (family history of Alzheimer's), certain genetic mutations, a history of head injuries, and cardiovascular risk factors such as high blood pressure, diabetes, and obesity.

Diagnosis

Diagnosing Alzheimer's disease involves a comprehensive assessment, including medical history, physical and neurological exams, cognitive testing, and sometimes brain imaging (such as MRI or CT scans). A definitive diagnosis often requires post-mortem examination of brain tissue.

Treatment

While there is currently no cure for Alzheimer's disease, some medications can help manage symptoms and slow the progression of the disease in some individuals. These medications may include cholinesterase inhibitors and memantine. Promising new medications are currently being studied but are not available currently. Non-pharmacological interventions, such as cognitive stimulation and lifestyle changes, can also be beneficial.

Caregiving

Alzheimer's disease places a significant burden on caregivers, as individuals with the disease require increasing levels of support and supervision. Caregivers play a crucial role in ensuring the safety and well-being of their loved ones with Alzheimer's.

Research and Hope

Ongoing research goals for Alzheimer's disease are to better understand its causes and develop more effective treatments. Early diagnosis and intervention can make a difference in managing the disease's progression and improving the quality of life for affected individuals.

Awareness and Advocacy

Alzheimer's organizations and advocates work tirelessly to raise awareness, provide support to caregivers, and promote research funding. World Alzheimer's Month is observed in September to raise global awareness of the disease.

Geriatric Depression: A Hidden Struggle

Geriatric depression, also known as late-life depression, refers to the occurrence of depressive symptoms or major depressive disorder in older adults, typically those aged 65 and above. It is a prevalent mental health issue among the elderly, but it is often underdiagnosed and undertreated, partially due to misconceptions that depression is a natural part of aging. However, geriatric depression is not a normal or inevitable consequence of getting older.

Differentiating geriatric depression involves recognizing symptoms such as:

- **Persistent sadness:** Prolonged periods of low mood, sadness, or hopelessness.

- **Social withdrawal:** Isolating oneself from social activities and family interactions.

- **Physical complaints:** Unexplained aches, pains, or digestive problems.

- **Cognitive changes:** Memory problems, difficulty concentrating, or a decline in decision-making ability.

- **Weight loss:** Significant changes in appetite and unexplained weight loss.

Prevalence

Geriatric depression is relatively common, affecting a significant portion of older adults. Prevalence studies suggest that between 14% to 20% of elderly individuals living in the community experience depressive symptoms, with higher rates in hospitalized or long-term care facility residents (Fiske et al., 2009).

Unique Challenges

Geriatric depression can present differently from depression in younger individuals. Older adults may be less likely to report classic depressive symptoms like sadness and may instead complain of physical symptoms such as fatigue, pain, or cognitive impairments.

Risk Factors

Several factors can increase the risk of depression in older adults, including a history of depression, chronic medical conditions, social isolation, loss of loved ones, and functional limitations.

Impact on Physical Health

Geriatric depression is not just a mental health concern; it can have a profound impact on physical health. It is associated with increased disability, worsened outcomes in chronic illnesses, and a higher risk of mortality.

Co-Occurrence

Geriatric depression often coexists with other medical conditions, such as heart disease, diabetes, and dementia, making it more challenging to diagnose and manage.

Screening and Diagnosis

Detecting geriatric depression may require specialized screening tools that consider the unique symptoms and presentation in older adults. Healthcare providers should be vigilant in assessing the mental well-being of their elderly patients.

Treatment

Treatment options for geriatric depression typically include psychotherapy (talk therapy) and, in some cases, medication. Antidepressants can be effective, but they should be used with caution, given the potential for interactions with other medications commonly prescribed to older adults.

Social Support

Social support from family, friends, and caregivers is crucial in managing geriatric depression. Loneliness and isolation can exacerbate depressive symptoms, so maintaining social connections is essential.

Prevention

Preventing geriatric depression involves addressing risk factors, promoting a healthy lifestyle, and ensuring that older adults have access to mental health care when needed.

Awareness and Education

Raising awareness about geriatric depression and dispelling myths about aging and mental health is essential. Family members and caregivers should be educated about the signs of depression in older adults and encouraged to seek professional help when necessary.

Geriatric depression is a significant mental health concern that affects many older adults. It is not a normal part of aging, and timely recognition and treatment are crucial to improving the well-being and quality of life of elderly individuals. If you or someone you know is experiencing symptoms of geriatric depression, it's essential to seek help from a healthcare professional or mental health specialist.

Knowledge Is Your Best Weapon

In the journey of caregiving for aging parents, knowledge serves as a powerful weapon against physical, emotional, and mental health risks. Understanding the signs and indicators of various health concerns empowers you to take prompt action when needed. Quick action can make all the difference, particularly in medical emergencies. Therefore, arming yourself with this knowledge ensures that you can provide the best care and support for your aging loved ones.

Chapter 4:

Addressing Legal Matters and Making Financial Decisions

While the journey of caring for aging parents is often fraught with emotional and physical challenges, there's a less talked-about but equally important aspect: the administrative side of aging. This chapter will explore estate planning, legal considerations, and assigning powers of attorney. Our goal is not merely to list these tasks but to underscore the necessity of open and direct communication between caregivers and their aging parents. This becomes especially significant if your parent is still able to engage in rational thought, logical reasoning, articulate speech, and comprehensive decision-making.

The Imperative of Administrative Preparations

When you step into the role of a caregiver, you are also unwittingly stepping into a myriad of roles—financial advisor, legal consultant, and often, the executor of last wishes. Many people are unprepared for this switch, and the consequences of poor planning can be severe.

Estate Planning

Think of estate planning as a roadmap for your aging parent's wishes. A well-drafted estate plan including wills, trusts, and beneficiary designations ensures that their assets are distributed as they wish after their passing. Without an estate plan, families have to address the difficulty of probate court, while also grieving their loss.

Legal Considerations

Another vital aspect is preparing legal documents such as power of attorney and healthcare proxies. These documents are critical as they designate someone to make important decisions when the aging parent cannot. It's not a decision to be made lightly, and it's certainly not one to be made without the consultation and consent of the parent, provided they are mentally capable.

Financial Decisions

Financial preparation is another cornerstone of graceful aging. This can range from investment plans aimed at sustaining quality of life to long-term care insurance. The decisions made here have long-term consequences and require thoughtful deliberation, ideally involving the parent in the process.

Why Communication Is Pivotal

This brings us to the crux of this chapter: communication. You may be wondering, "Why is it so vital?"

- **Inclusion and respect:** Involving your aging parent in these discussions respects their agency and includes them in decisions that directly affect their life and legacy.

- **Clarity and understanding:** Open dialogue ensures that everyone is on the same page, avoiding misunderstandings that can lead to familial disputes later.

- **Shared responsibility:** Decision-making becomes a shared responsibility, providing the caregiver with the much-needed emotional support and the parent with a sense of control and dignity.

- **Professional guidance:** After initial conversations, caregivers and parents should jointly consult professionals to ensure that all plans align with current laws and best practices.

The Cautionary Tale of Krysten Crawford

Sometimes, life offers us poignant lessons through the experiences of others. One such cautionary tale is that of Krysten Crawford, a story that echoes the complexities and urgency of addressing the administrative side of aging. As detailed in a *New York Times* article, Krysten found herself in a labyrinth of financial and legal troubles, all stemming from a seemingly simple issue: a delayed death certificate for her deceased mother (Tugend, 2019).

A Tangled Web

Krysten's mother had recently passed away, and like many grieving families, she and her siblings were consumed with the emotional toll it took. While they did expect some administrative tasks, they were unprepared for the avalanche of complications that followed. One critical element that got delayed was the death certificate. This document, generally considered a straightforward piece of paper, suddenly became the linchpin holding up numerous crucial transactions.

The Domino Effect

The delay in obtaining the death certificate created a cascade of issues. This single document was needed for a multitude of legal and financial processes, from gaining access to her mother's bank accounts to settling life insurance policies. Without it, Krysten and her siblings found themselves unable to make timely payments on the mortgage for their mother's house. This led to a downward spiral of accumulating late fees, penalties, and an increasing risk of foreclosure.

The Price of Unpreparedness

Krysten's experience reveals the layers of complexity involved in managing the affairs of a deceased parent. What's striking is that the absence of one single document could throw multiple aspects of their lives into disarray. It serves as a stark reminder of the importance of not only knowing what needs to be done when a parent ages or passes away but being proactive in managing those details.

Money Talks: The Critical Importance of Financial Conversations With Aging Parents

The story of Krysten Crawford not only serves as a cautionary tale but also opens the door to a crucial dialogue that many of us avoid: the financial matters related to aging parents. Many elderly individuals live off a fixed income, consisting of savings and pension plans, lacking the financial flexibility that comes from a steady income stream. Even if you are in a position to financially support your parents, there are specific topics that you absolutely must discuss with them, one of which is the healthcare budget.

The Concept of a Healthcare Budget

When we talk about a healthcare budget, we refer to the allocation of funds designated for medical expenses. This can range from hospital stays and regular check-ups to ongoing medications and specialized treatments. These are recurring financial commitments that can significantly impact your parents' overall budget.

Why It's Important to Discuss

Healthcare costs can quickly escalate, becoming a major financial burden. Furthermore, it's common for aging individuals to have multiple health issues requiring different forms of medical intervention. Understanding your parents' healthcare budget will provide insights into how well-prepared they are for unforeseen medical costs. Knowing the budget can also help when making choices about treatments, medications, and healthcare providers. Lastly, it serves as a useful parameter for you, the caregiver, in gauging the level of financial support you might need to provide.

Learning From Trusted Sources

For comprehensive advice on this matter, it may be useful to refer to the following resources:

A *Forbes* article by Carolyn Rosenblatt (2021b) discusses smart ways to talk to aging parents about their finances. Rosenblatt emphasizes the need for a delicate yet direct approach, suggesting that professional financial advice might be helpful.

F&G Life's blog post focuses on the importance of timing when initiating these discussions (Rosenblatt, 2013). The article advises readers to talk to their parents sooner rather than later, ideally when they are still in good health and of sound mind.

Emergency Funds: A Safety Net for Unforeseen Circumstances

What Is an Emergency Fund?

An emergency fund serves as a financial cushion for unexpected life events, such as medical emergencies, unforeseen debts, or sudden living expenses. In the context of aging parents, these funds become even more crucial. The primary question here is: Do your parents have a separate stash of money put aside to deal with emergencies? If so, how much? And are they open to letting you contribute to this fund?

Why an Emergency Fund Is Crucial for Aging Parents

The need for an emergency fund intensifies as one ages, mainly due to increased health risks and potential for unplanned expenses. For aging parents, an emergency fund is not just good to have; it's essential. According to an article on GetCarefull, having an emergency fund can provide peace of mind and financial security, allowing retirees to deal with unexpected situations without destabilizing their financial well-being (Freedman, 2023).

Similar articles from The Balance Money, The Motley Fool, and Yahoo Finance echo the need for retirees to maintain a robust emergency fund. These funds can vary in size but should be substantial enough to cover at least 3-6 months' worth of living expenses.

On-Going Payments: Keeping Tabs on Recurring Expenditures

The Nature of On-Going Payments

As your parents age, they may find themselves entangled in a web of recurring payments, ranging from utility bills and insurance premiums to magazine subscriptions and club memberships. Understanding the landscape of these on-going payments is crucial for several reasons, and it may be worth sitting down with your parents to review which of these payments are necessary and which can be eliminated to increase savings.

Why This Discussion Is Important

Managing finances gets more complicated with age, and your parents may not be keeping a close eye on all their recurring payments. Unnecessary expenditures can quickly add up, depleting resources that could be better used elsewhere or saved for emergencies. According to an article in The Balance Money, having this financial discussion can be a cornerstone of effective financial planning (Bond, 2022).

In *The News Herald*, experts recommend creating a list of all ongoing payments as a starting point for financial management (Bumgardner, 2023). And, as emphasized in *The New York Times*, transparent communication about finances between aging parents and their children is essential for both parties' financial well-being (Bernard, 2013). Both emergency funds and ongoing payments are critical aspects of your parents' financial life that require your attention and proactive management. Failing to address these topics could put your parents at financial risk and add stress to an already emotionally charged phase of life. With careful planning and open communication, however, you can help ensure that your parents' financial future is as secure as possible.

Future Financial Plans: A Blueprint for Longevity and Legacy

The Importance of Discussing Future Financial Plans

Just because your parents are aging doesn't mean they should neglect planning for the future. These plans could range from future care options and living situations to estate planning, charitable giving, and legacies they may want to leave behind. Having a candid conversation about these plans can offer clarity and help families prepare for various scenarios, thereby avoiding potential misunderstandings later. According to various sources like the *New York Times*, CNBC, and Money Geek, such financial planning is critical for a secure and fulfilling future for aging parents.

How to Approach the Topic: Guidelines for a Respectful Conversation

Having a conversation about finances and legal matters with your aging parents can be a delicate task. While it's a topic that needs to be addressed, the approach matters significantly. Here are some guidelines on how to initiate and sustain a meaningful discussion:

Be Direct

It's easy to get caught up in the legalese and financial jargon but remember: simplicity is key. Use straightforward language and avoid confusing terms or hypothetical situations. Your goal is to make the topic digestible and less intimidating for your parents. For instance, instead of saying, "We need to discuss your posthumous financial disbursements," you might say, "Let's talk about how you'd like to handle your money and property after you're gone."

Timing Is Everything

The timing of the conversation is crucial. This is not a chat to have in the midst of a birthday celebration, holiday gathering, or any special event where emotions are already running high. Choose a quiet, comfortable setting where everyone can focus on the matter at hand. You might even consider informing your parents ahead of time that you'd like to discuss this, so they have a chance to prepare mentally.

Approach With Love and Respect

Your demeanor and tone of voice can make all the difference. Approach the conversation from a place of love, respect, and concern for your parents' well-being. This isn't a business meeting; it's a family discussion. Let them know that you're bringing this up not to control their lives but to help ensure their comfort and security in their later years.

Choose Your Words Carefully

The vocabulary you use can set the stage for how the conversation unfolds. Be respectful, empathetic, and compassionate in your choice of words. Rather than saying, "You need to do this," perhaps frame it as, "It might be a good idea to consider these options for your peace of mind and ours."

Be Considerate

Before diving into the discussion, take a moment to consider how you would feel if your roles were reversed. Be sensitive to your parents' potential fears or hesitations about discussing such intimate matters. Ask yourself how you'd like to be approached if you were in their shoes and try to emulate that respect and tactfulness.

Compromise in Case of Disagreement

Disagreements are bound to happen. Your parents have lived long lives with their own sets of beliefs and values. If you encounter resistance or differing views, aim for a compromise that respects their autonomy while also ensuring their long-term well-being.

Gentle Questions in Case of Resistance

If you're meeting resistance, don't resort to pressure tactics. Instead, gently probe to better understand where their concerns lie. Questions like, "Is there a specific reason you're uncomfortable talking about this?" or "What worries you most about this topic?" can help illuminate their hesitations and give you a better basis for discussion.

Approaching the topic of financial planning and legal representation with your aging parents is not just about what you say but how you say it. The goal is to build a collaborative and respectful dialogue that benefits everyone involved. If needed, refer to expert advice from the resources provided to help guide these critical conversations.

For further reading and tips, consult reliable sources like Kiplinger, The Guardian Life, Daily Caring, and VHA.

Conversations about future financial plans are vital for both your peace of mind and that of your aging parents. These talks can be emotionally charged and challenging but are essential for avoiding confusion and potential disputes down the line. It's a proactive approach that helps ensure the financial well-being of your parents and provides a clear roadmap for how to handle various scenarios that may arise in the future. Effective communication, done respectfully and thoughtfully, can make all the difference.

Legal Representation: Considerations for Aging Parents

When taking on the responsibility of caring for aging parents, there's a broad spectrum of concerns that extend beyond immediate health and emotional well-being. As a caregiver, you also enter the complex world of legal and financial planning, which involves various elements such as trust funds, wills, power of attorney, and property ownership. These legal facets are not just paperwork; they're crucial instruments for safeguarding your parents' future, protecting their assets, and clearly defining their wishes and legacies.

Addressing these matters proactively can mitigate potential conflicts, provide a roadmap for future care, and offer peace of mind for everyone involved in this often-emotional journey. For in-depth insights and advice, sources like NBC News, AARP, and JD Supra offer comprehensive guides on how to address these vital issues.

Power of Attorney

What Is It?

A Power of Attorney (POA) is a legal document that grants one individual—the "agent"—the authority to act on behalf of another person—the "principal"—in various situations that can range from financial matters to healthcare decisions. This authority can be as broad or as specific as the principal chooses, allowing the agent to manage bank accounts, sign contracts, make medical decisions, and more.

Why Is It Important?

Having a Power of Attorney (POA) in place is crucial, especially for aging parents, as it acts as a safety net for unforeseen circumstances where they may become incapacitated or unable to make rational decisions on their own. Designating a POA can serve as a pre-emptive measure to avoid the often complex, time-consuming, and costly legal process of court-appointed guardianship.

Having this legal document ready can minimize the potential for family disagreements and legal entanglements that could arise in emotionally charged situations. It offers clarity and structure, ensuring that your parents' wishes are respected and acted upon should they become unable to communicate or make decisions themselves.

Estate Planning

What Is It?

Estate planning is a comprehensive legal process that encompasses the planned distribution of an individual's assets, such as properties, financial accounts, investments, and personal belongings, after their death. It often involves the creation of various legal documents like wills, trusts, and power of attorney agreements. But it's not just about transferring assets; it can also include arrangements for healthcare decisions, care for dependents, and even funeral preparations.

Why Is It Important?

The importance of estate planning, especially for aging parents, cannot be overstated. Having a comprehensive estate plan in place ensures that your parents' wishes are carried out after their death, eliminating the guesswork and potential conflict among surviving family members. It can also minimize taxes, legal expenses, and court fees, thus preserving the estate's value for its intended beneficiaries.

Discussing these matters while your parents are still mentally competent is crucial, as waiting too long could lead to situations where their wishes may not be adequately communicated or executed, resulting in legal complications or family disagreements.

Well-crafted estate planning can also provide safeguards against potential exploitation or financial abuse, an unfortunate risk the elderly often face. It sets the stage for a smoother transition of assets and responsibilities, lessening the emotional and financial burden on the family during an already difficult time.

Legal Documents Checklist

Caring for an elderly parent often involves more than just emotional and physical support; it also requires a thorough understanding of legal considerations to ensure their well-being. Here's a detailed list of legal documents you should consider having in place, categorized for easier understanding:

Financial Documents

- **General durable power of attorney (POA):** Allows you to manage your parent's financial affairs, including paying bills and managing investments, if they become incapacitated.

- **Bank account authorizations:** Gives you permission to access and manage your parent's bank accounts.

- **Retirement accounts:** Documents related to IRAs, 401(k)s, and other retirement accounts, including beneficiary designations.

Healthcare Documents

- **Healthcare power of attorney (POA):** Lets you make medical decisions on your parent's behalf if they can't do so themselves.

- **Living will/advanced health care directive:** Specifies your parent's preferences for end-of-life medical care.

- **HIPAA authorization:** Allows healthcare providers to share your parent's medical information with you.

- **Medical records:** A comprehensive file of medical history, medications, doctors' contacts, and so on.

End-of-Life Planning Documents

- **Last will and testament:** Specifies how your parent's assets will be distributed after their death.

- **Revocable living trust:** Allows assets to pass outside of probate. This can be especially useful if your parent owns property in more than one state.

- **Funeral arrangements:** Details of desired funeral or memorial services, including burial or cremation preferences.

- **Digital asset inventory:** A list of digital assets like social media accounts, digital photos, and online banking accounts, along with instructions for how to access them.

Miscellaneous Documents

- **Real estate deeds and mortgage papers:** Papers related to property ownership.

- **Vehicle titles and registration:** Documents related to owned vehicles.

- **Insurance policies:** Information related to life, health, property, and other types of insurance.

- **Social security records:** Information on social security benefits.

- **Tax records:** Past tax returns and related documents.

Ensure that these documents are stored in a secure but accessible location, and that relevant family members or advisors know where to find them. It's also advisable to consult with an elder law attorney to make sure that all documents are in order, up-to-date, and in compliance with current state laws.

In addition to ensuring all the paperwork is in order, we must also prepare for conversations that may be emotionally challenging but are incredibly necessary. The next chapter will delve into the second part of this guide: communicating with your parents about sensitive topics like deteriorating health and end-of-life wishes.

Chapter 5:

The Importance of Communication, Part 2: Medical Matters and Sensitive Topics

We continue our discussion about the importance of communication with your aging parents. The goal here is to address topics that, although delicate, are essential: end-of-life wishes, funeral arrangements, medical preferences, and the like. This chapter provides you with the tools and advice you'll need to approach these matters in a sensitive yet open manner, as well as how to cope with the emotional toll such conversations may take.

When I was 27, I had an encounter with my 91-year-old grandmother that would stay with me forever. During a visit, she suddenly started talking about the various furniture pieces she owned and asked me to pick out a few that I would like to have when she was gone. It was a bit of an awkward turn in the conversation, to say the least.

"Ah, well, I do like that cabinet over there," I mumbled.

"Oh, your brother already claimed that one," she said cheerfully.

"How about that coffee table?" I tried again.

"Your sister wants that," she replied.

I was getting frustrated. It felt like the estate sale had already happened, and I was late to the party. Just as I was about to express my annoyance, my grandmother caught my eye and smiled warmly.

"Don't worry," she said. "You'll get something special because you are special. Everything that's left will have your name on it, because you cared to ask and cared to listen."

That reassurance shifted the whole tone of our conversation. The very topic that had seemed so grave and upsetting became a lighthearted discussion about her favorite antiques. And, at that moment, I realized the discussion wasn't really about furniture at all. It was about legacy, memories, and love, wrapped in the complex emotions that only conversations about end-of-life can bring.

That day taught me two crucial lessons about discussing sensitive topics like death and future plans. First, expect emotions to run high—whether it's frustration, sadness, or even relief. Second, as awkward as it might seem to bring up these subjects, doing so opens the door to profound emotional connection and understanding.

The story highlights the complex emotions tied to end-of-life conversations. It's a topic that might be riddled with emotional outbursts, but it also offers a kind of closure, peace, and even unexpected humor. When approached right, talking about such issues can be a rewarding experience for everyone involved.

In this section, we'll discuss how to approach these conversations with sensitivity and planning. We'll also cover specific topics you should discuss and provide guidance on how to handle any emotional turbulence you might encounter along the way. So, let's get started.

Advanced Care Directives

What Is an Advanced Care Directive?

An Advanced Care Directive is a legal document that outlines a person's wishes regarding their medical treatment, especially treatments they would or would not want to receive in case they are unable to communicate their decisions due to severe illness or incapacitation. These directives can cover a range of issues, from resuscitation efforts to preferences about end-of-life care, including whether to administer pain medications, antibiotics, or even whether to use feeding tubes.

These documents are often part of a broader estate planning process and serve as a guide for healthcare providers and family members responsible for making medical decisions on the individual's behalf.

Why Is an Advanced Care Directive Important?

Discussing the importance of an Advanced Care Directive with your aging parents is not just a procedural formality; it's an act of compassion and foresight. Several reasons make this document essential:

- **Clarity in crisis:** In situations where immediate medical decisions are required, an Advanced Care Directive eliminates guesswork, providing clear guidance to healthcare providers and family members.

- **Respecting wishes:** This document ensures that your parents' wishes regarding their healthcare are respected, even if they are unable to articulate them at that moment.

- **Avoiding family conflict:** In the absence of an Advanced Care Directive, family members might have differing opinions on the "best" course of action, leading to emotional conflicts at an already stressful time.

- **Legal safeguard:** An Advanced Care Directive serves as a legal document that healthcare providers are obliged to follow, ensuring that medical treatments align with your parents' preferences.

- **Emotional peace:** Knowing that there is a plan in place can offer emotional relief to both parents and adult children, making an inherently difficult time slightly easier to handle.

So, if your parents haven't yet secured an Advanced Care Directive, it's imperative to encourage them to do so. It's not an easy topic to discuss, but it's a necessary one. *The Forbes* article titled "Smart Ways to Talk to Aging Parents About Finances" advises making these discussions a routine part of ongoing conversations about planning for the future, thereby making them less intimidating and more natural (Rosenblatt, 2013).

Given the high stakes and the emotional weight these directives carry, the time to act is now—when your parents are still capable of making these decisions for themselves. Not only does it protect their autonomy, but it also provides a roadmap for you and other family members to follow when the situation calls for it.

Emotionally Sensitive Topics

Facing Uncomfortable Truths

Talking about sensitive subjects like end-of-life plans, funeral arrangements, or declining health is never easy, for you or for your aging parents. It's particularly challenging when you have a close relationship, and your parents appear to be in good health for their age. The instinct to avoid these conversations is natural and understandable; after all, who wants to think about such grim eventualities when things are going well?

The Price of Denial

While optimism about your parents' well-being is commendable, it should not prevent critical conversations from taking place. Denial, while a natural emotional response, can create long-term challenges. Avoiding these topics can lead to heightened confusion and emotional turmoil at the times when you and your family can least afford it—during moments of crisis or grief.

Topics We Will Cover

Although the range of sensitive topics could be quite extensive, this section will focus on key areas that, despite their emotional heaviness, are crucial to address. These include:

End-of-Life Wishes

The Questions You Should Ask

When discussing end-of-life plans, it's crucial to go beyond medical and financial logistics to touch on more personal matters. Does your parent have specific places they want to visit before their time is up? Are there gifts they wish to give in person, or perhaps a long-lost friend or family member with whom they'd like to reconnect or reconcile? Discussing these details can be emotionally taxing but is essential for a holistic understanding of your parent's wishes.

The Importance of This Discussion

The topic of end-of-life wishes goes beyond ensuring that legal and medical procedures are followed; it taps into the emotional and spiritual aspects of life and legacy. Discussing these matters can be a profound experience that brings satisfaction and a sense of closure to both parties involved. People who have these conversations earlier and more openly are less likely to suffer from stress and depression during the end-of-life process. They are also more likely to feel that their life had meaning and purpose, thereby improving their quality of life even in its final stages.

Mutual Benefits for Parent and Child

For your parents, knowing that their specific wishes will be honored can bring a sense of peace and resolution. They can focus on living their remaining days according to their terms, with the knowledge that their affairs are in order.

As for you, the adult child, these conversations can alleviate the burden of having to make challenging decisions during emotionally charged times. You'll gain the reassurance that you're acting in line with your parents' true wishes, reducing the risk of family conflicts that can often arise under such circumstances.

Legal Documents

What Is a Formal Will?

A formal will is a legal document that outlines how an individual's assets and estate will be distributed after their death. This is a critical document that should ideally be drafted and validated legally to ensure that your parent's wishes are followed in the event of their passing. There are several types of formal wills, each suited for different needs:

- **Simple Will:** A straightforward document that outlines who will receive your assets and properties.

- **Testamentary Trust Will:** This includes provisions that create a trust upon the testator's death.

- **Joint Will:** Created by two people, usually spouses, to leave their assets to each other.

- **Online Will:** Created and stored online but must still meet legal criteria to be valid.

- **Deathbed Will:** Created when a person knows they are about to die soon, typically handwritten and witnessed.

- **Holographic Will:** Handwritten and signed by the person making the will, without witnesses. Its legality varies by jurisdiction.

- **Nuncupative Will:** An oral will, usually made before witnesses but not recommended as it can be difficult to validate.

The Importance of a Formal Will

If your parents haven't already drafted a formal will, it is imperative to encourage them to do so. A formal will ensures that there is no ambiguity in the distribution of assets and reduces the potential for family conflict during an emotionally fraught time. Furthermore, it is legally binding and offers the most secure way to carry out your parents' final wishes.

What Is an Informal Will?

An informal will is not typically drafted with the help of legal professionals and may not meet all the formal requirements laid down by law. These are sometimes handwritten notes or even digital messages that express a person's wishes regarding the distribution of their estate.

When Could an Informal Will Be Useful?

While it's most advisable for your parents to have a formal will, an informal will can serve as a stopgap in certain circumstances. If your parent passes away before they can have their will legally checked and validated, an informal will may still provide some direction regarding their wishes. While not ideal, an informal will is better than having no will at all, as it may offer some guidance and reduce conflicts among surviving family members.

While a formal will offers the most legal security and clarity, having an informal will is better than having no documentation at all regarding your parents' wishes for their estate. However, the best course of action is to ensure that a formal will is in place as soon as possible.

Funeral and Burial Arrangements: The Emotional Weight of the Topic

Discussing funeral arrangements is undoubtedly one of the more emotionally heavy conversations you'll need to have with your aging parents. The very topic evokes a visceral realization of mortality, both for you and your parents. That said, it is a necessary conversation that, when approached with sensitivity and understanding, can provide everyone with peace of mind. Take a deep breath; it's okay. You're not alone, and this is a topic that many adult children must eventually face with their parents. In some cases, you may even find that your parent brings up the subject first.

The Importance of Discussing Funeral Arrangements

Although it's a difficult topic, discussing funeral arrangements is a crucial step in preparing for the inevitable future. Having this discussion beforehand allows for planning and organization that will make a challenging time slightly more manageable for the family left behind. The absence of such conversations can lead to unnecessary stress and disagreements among family members during an already emotionally fraught period.

How to Broach the Topic

If you find yourself initiating this conversation, it's beneficial to pick an appropriate time when both you and your parents are not already emotionally overwhelmed. Approach the topic gently, perhaps starting with broader end-of-life discussions and narrowing down to funeral arrangements. Be prepared for a range of emotional reactions; some parents may find relief in finally talking about it, while others may initially resist the conversation.

Key Points to Cover

- Have they discussed their preferred funeral arrangements with anyone?

- What type of funeral? Religious, non-religious, or spiritual?

- Do they have any specific preferences regarding ceremonies, readings, or music?

- Do they have preferences regarding burial or cremation services?

- If they want to be buried, do they already have a plot in a cemetery?

- If they want to be buried but don't have a plot yet, do they have a specific cemetery/place in mind?

- Are there any existing plans or insurance policies that cover funeral costs?

Closure for Everyone

Though emotionally taxing, these conversations can often bring an unexpected sense of relief and closure, both for you and your parents. It ensures that their wishes are known and will be respected, and it leaves you with one less thing to worry about when the time comes.

Take the step, have the conversation, and know that you're doing the best you can to honor your parents' wishes.

- **Medical care preferences:** Discussing what kinds of treatments your parents would prefer or avoid in various scenarios can be eye-opening and is essential for everyone involved.

- **Financial and legal aspects:** While this was covered in the previous chapter, it often intertwines with emotionally sensitive topics.

- **Legacy and possessions:** This may involve discussing who gets what in terms of family heirlooms, property, and other valuable items.

Possible Resistance

Conversations with aging parents about sensitive issues like health, legal matters, and end-of-life plans can often be met with resistance. It's not uncommon for older adults to resist discussing these critical topics, insisting on maintaining their current ways or opinions. According to research, this resistance may come from various emotional factors, including pride, fear, or a need to maintain control (Lerner et al., 2015).

These difficult conversations requires a thoughtful approach. "Understanding why parents may be ... insisting, resisting, or persisting in their ways or opinions ... can lead to better communication," advises one expert (Lerner et al., 2015). Furthermore, Zarit, another expert in the field, provides invaluable guidance: "Do not pick arguments. Do not make a parent feel defensive. Plant an idea, step back, and bring it up later. Be patient" (Berman, 2016).

For those finding it especially difficult to engage their parents in these discussions, several strategies can help. Show empathy and try to understand the emotions affecting your parents. Use non-confrontational language, and maybe bring in a neutral third party like a medical professional to provide a different perspective.

While it's easy to become frustrated, remember that this is a delicate subject for your parents as well. Patience, empathy, and careful timing can go a long way in facilitating meaningful and productive conversations.

Emotional and Mental Health

- What are their views on psychological counseling or therapy? Are they open to it should a situation arise that warrants mental health support?

- Have they ever talked about signs of depression or anxiety, and would they be open to discussing a plan should either become a concern?

- How do they feel about psychiatric medications? Would they be willing to take them if recommended?

- Who do they want to talk to in difficult emotional times? Do they have a preferred point of contact?

End-of-Life Wishes

- Do they have any thoughts on what kind of end-of-life care they would like to receive?

- How do they feel about hospice care?

- Do they have specific religious or spiritual rituals they want observed at the end of their life?

Family Relationships and Dynamics

- Are there any unresolved family issues they wish to address?

- How do they feel about family counseling?

- Is there any specific information or advice they want to pass down to family members?

Digital and Social Media Footprint

- What should be done with their email accounts, social media profiles, and other digital assets after they pass away?

- Do they have a list of passwords and account information in a safe place?

Organ Donation and Medical Research

- What are their views on organ donation?

- Would they be willing to donate their body for medical research?

Pet Care

- If they have pets, what arrangements would they like to make for their care?

Business and Investments

- Do they have any ongoing business ventures that need to be managed or terminated?

- How would they like their investments to be managed?

Personal Possessions

- What should be done with their personal belongings?

- Are there specific items they want to pass down to certain individuals?

Additional Concerns and Preferences

- Are there certain doctors, caregivers, or institutions they prefer for health care?

- Do they have any dietary restrictions or preferences that should be honored in medical or palliative care?

These topics may be difficult to discuss, but they are essential conversations to have with your parents. It's better to know their wishes and be prepared than to be uncertain in times of crisis. The sooner you address these questions, the better you'll be able to respect and fulfill your parents' wishes should the need arise. Always approach these topics with sensitivity, empathy, and openness.

Remember, there are professionals who specialize in guiding these types of discussions. If you or your parents find it too difficult to talk about these topics directly, consider seeking the assistance of counselors, attorneys, or medical professionals. Check the "Additional Resources" section for more information on who can help.

Chapter 6:

Self-Care for Caregivers, Part 1: Making Space for Self-Healing

Caring for an aging or ill family member is a physically, psychologically, and emotionally demanding job. While the act of caregiving can be rewarding, it also often leads to caregiver burnout—a state of emotional, mental, and physical exhaustion. To be able to provide the best care possible, caregivers must remember to take care of themselves too. This chapter provides actionable advice on how to maintain your health and manage stress so that you can be a better caregiver for your aging parent.

Some sobering statistics regarding caregivers (APA, 2011):

- According to the American Psychological Association, about 55% of family caregivers report feeling overwhelmed by the amount of care their aging family member needs.

- AARP reports that one in five caregivers say their health has gotten worse because of their caregiving responsibilities.

- The Family Caregiver Alliance notes that 60-70% of family caregivers show clinically significant symptoms of depression.

- According to the Centers for Disease Control and Prevention (CDC), caregivers for the elderly are twice as likely as the general population to report chronic conditions like heart disease, diabetes, or arthritis.

- Research published in the *Journal of Gerontology* indicates that caregivers have a 23% higher level of stress hormones compared to non-caregivers.

- A study by the Proceedings of the National Academy of Sciences suggests that caregivers experiencing extreme stress age prematurely, showing aging markers that are equivalent to being 9-17 years older.

- The National Alliance for Caregiving reports that 17% of caregivers feel their health in general has become worse because of their caregiving responsibilities.

You Can't Pour from an Empty Cup: The Reality of Caregiver Stress and Burnout

The adage "you can't pour from an empty cup" holds particularly true for caregivers. When you're worn down both physically and emotionally, your ability to provide quality care diminishes. Caregiver stress and burnout are not just buzzwords; they are pressing health concerns that can affect your well-being and the quality of care you provide.

The phenomenon of caregiver burnout is both perplexing and all too common, especially among adult children caring for elderly parents. While it may seem counterintuitive, many caregivers seem resigned to the idea of wearing themselves thin, succumbing to exhaustion both mentally and physically. There are several contributing factors that fuel this unfortunate mindset.

Firstly, the overwhelming sense of duty that adult children often feel towards their aging parents can be a double-edged sword. While this responsibility may drive them to provide the best care possible, it often comes at the sacrifice of their own well-being. The cultural or familial expectation that they "owe" it to their parents to be the primary caregivers can make it difficult to step back and recognize their own needs.

Secondly, guilt plays a significant role in caregiver burnout. Caregivers often grapple with the idea that taking time for themselves equates to neglecting their elderly loved ones. This emotional burden can become an unending cycle, as the more worn out the caregivers are, the less effective they can be in their caregiving roles—which, in turn, amplifies their feelings of guilt.

Thirdly, lack of resources exacerbates the situation. Whether due to financial constraints, limited access to professional support, or simply not knowing where to turn for help, many caregivers find themselves feeling isolated and unsupported. This lack of a support system makes them more vulnerable to stress, fatigue, and, eventually, complete burnout.

Lastly, denial is a dangerous contributor to caregiver burnout. Many caregivers underestimate the toll that constant caregiving can take on their physical and emotional health. They often push through the exhaustion, thinking it's a phase that will pass, only to realize too late that they are experiencing the full-blown symptoms of burnout.

Understanding these factors is crucial for breaking the cycle and making self-care a priority in the caregiving journey.

Caregiver Stress and Burnout

The terms "caregiver stress" and "caregiver burnout" are often used interchangeably, but they represent distinct stages of emotional and physical toll. Caregiver stress refers to the initial emotional and physical strain that comes with caregiving responsibilities. This stress manifests in a range of symptoms from anxiety and depression to irritability, and even physical issues such as headaches and insomnia.

Caregiver burnout, on the other hand, signifies a more advanced state of exhaustion encompassing physical, emotional, and mental fatigue. It goes beyond stress to include symptoms like diminished energy, weakened immunity, and a growing disinterest not only in the caregiving role but, alarmingly, in life itself.

Exploring the Ripple Effects of Stress and Burnout

When it comes to the consequences of stress and burnout, the ramifications extend far beyond the caregiver's well-being. For the caregiver, enduring chronic stress may escalate into severe health complications, including hypertension, diabetes, and a weakened immune system. Additionally, the emotional toll can manifest as heightened anxiety, deepening depression, and an overall reduction in quality of life.

As for the patient, a caregiver's stress and burnout have been proven to compromise the quality of care they receive. The ramifications can be severe, ranging from unintentional neglect to more serious medical errors. Recognizing the symptoms and impact of caregiver stress and burnout is crucial, not only for the well-being of the caregiver but for the safety and health of the person they are caring for.

Stress and burnout manifest in both physical and psychological ways. Recognizing the signs early on is critical for taking steps to mitigate their effects. Here's an in-depth look:

Physical Signs

- **Chronic fatigue:** Feeling tired is one thing, but if you find that you're perpetually exhausted, even after a good night's sleep, it may be a sign of burnout. Chronic fatigue can seriously affect your ability to care for someone else effectively.

- **Frequent illness:** Stress weakens the immune system, making you more susceptible to colds, flu, and other infections. If you find that you're getting sick more often than usual, it could be due to elevated stress levels.

- **Headaches or migraines:** A constant, unexplained headache or more severe migraines can be indicators of chronic stress or the beginning stages of burnout.

- **Gastrointestinal issues:** Problems like heartburn, acid reflux, or irritable bowel syndrome can worsen with stress.

Emotional Signs

- **Increased irritability:** Minor annoyances become major issues, and you may find yourself snapping at the person you're caring for or others around you. This heightened irritability can strain relationships and decrease the quality of care you provide.

- **Anxiety and worry:** Excessive worrying about the future, feeling tense, or experiencing generalized anxiety that impacts your daily functioning may signal stress or impending burnout.

- **Depression:** Persistent feelings of sadness, worthlessness, and hopelessness can be severe signs of emotional exhaustion and burnout.

- **Detachment:** If you find yourself becoming emotionally detached from the person you are caring for, or from your own loved ones, it's a significant red flag.

Behavioral Signs

- **Decreased performance:** If tasks that were once simple for you suddenly become difficult and overwhelming, this could be a sign that stress and burnout are taking a toll.

- **Avoidance:** Escaping responsibilities or avoiding necessary interactions with the care recipient, friends, or family members is a sign that something is wrong.

- **Changes in appetite or sleep patterns:** Eating too much or too little, insomnia, or sleeping too much can all be signs of stress or burnout.

- **Substance abuse:** Increased reliance on alcohol, recreational drugs, or even prescription medications to get through the day is a serious indicator of high stress and possible burnout.

Cognitive Signs

- **Memory problems:** Difficulty in remembering important dates, tasks, or even trivial everyday details can signal stress or burnout.

- **Indecisiveness:** If making even small decisions starts to feel overwhelming, it could be due to cognitive strain brought on by stress.

- **Reduced concentration:** An inability to focus during essential tasks not only compromises the quality of care you're providing but also is a classic symptom of stress and burnout.

Making Time for Self-Care

You owe it to yourself and your parent to maintain your well-being. Here are some steps to prevent stress and burnout:

- **Recognize the signs:** Being aware of your physical and emotional state is the first step.

- **Ask for help:** Whether it's from friends, family, or professionals, don't shy away from asking for help.

- **Set boundaries:** It's okay to say no or delegate tasks.

- **Time management:** Make time for activities that nourish your body and soul.

- **The importance of balance:** Navigating between caregiving and personal time.

The emotional weight and physical demands of caregiving can easily make it a full-time job, eclipsing other aspects of your life. Striking a balance between the time you dedicate to caring for your parents and your personal needs is crucial for your own well-being and for providing quality care.

The Myth of the 24/7 Caregiver

Firstly, let's dispel a common myth: you cannot and should not be "on-call" 24/7. Being constantly available for caregiving duties is not only impractical but also detrimental to your health and personal life. Whether you have a day job, hobbies, personal projects, or a social circle, these aspects of your life also deserve attention and nourishment.

The Conversation: Open Dialogue with Your Parents

Open communication with your parents about the need for balance is essential. Reference back to the previous chapters on effective communication; this is another subject that needs to be discussed openly and honestly. Let your parents know that balancing your personal life with caregiving duties isn't a sign of neglect but a necessary step for holistic well-being.

Tips for Achieving Balance

- **Prioritize tasks:** Identify the caregiving tasks that only you can do and those that can be handled by others or through professional services.

- **Seek help:** Enlist other family members or hire professional services for some of the caregiving responsibilities.

- **Set time limits:** Allocate specific hours of the day for caregiving tasks and stick to them as much as possible.

- **Time for yourself:** Block out periods in your day or week for personal activities, whether it's going to the gym, reading, or spending time with friends.

- **Be flexible but firm:** Life is unpredictable; while you need to be flexible to some extent, being firm about your boundaries is equally important.

The Challenge for Live-in Caregivers

For adult children who have moved back home to care for their parents, achieving balance is even more challenging. Being around your ward 24/7 may make it difficult to delineate caregiving time from personal time. This underscores the necessity to set strong boundaries, which we'll delve into in the next section.

Setting Boundaries: A Necessary Measure for Caregivers and Parents Alike

Establishing boundaries is not only one of the most effective ways to preserve your mental health but also essential for maintaining a healthy relationship with your aging parents. Let's look deeper into why this is so crucial and how best to go about it.

The Non-Negotiable Need for Boundaries

Setting boundaries is non-negotiable. While the emotional and physical demands of caregiving may seem endless, your energy and emotional reserves are not. Boundaries delineate personal time for rest, recreation, and self-care. This designated time is essential for rejuvenating your spirit and body, ensuring you can provide quality care for your aging parent.

Communicating Your Boundaries

When you start setting boundaries, clear communication with your parents is vital. It may be a challenging conversation, but it's one that can't be avoided. Be transparent about your needs, and make sure they understand that these boundaries are not only for your benefit but, ultimately, for theirs as well. A well-rested and mentally healthy caregiver is far more effective than an exhausted one.

Practical Tips for Boundary-Setting

- **Be specific:** Vagueness is the enemy when it comes to boundaries. Be as precise as possible about what you can and cannot do.

- **Be consistent:** Once you set a boundary, make sure you stick to it. Consistency is key for your parents to understand and respect your limits.

- **Involve other family members:** Don't try to shoulder all the responsibilities yourself. Delegate tasks to other family members or professional caregivers as needed.

- **Periodic review:** Life circumstances can change, which means your boundaries may need to be adjusted. Make it a point to periodically review and revise them.

- **Prepare for resistance:** Your parents may initially resist or react negatively to the new boundaries. Be prepared for this and stay firm in your commitment.

The Long-Term Benefits

By setting effective boundaries, you're safeguarding yourself from the debilitating effects of caregiver burnout, a phenomenon well-documented in multiple studies and articles. Moreover, you're also modeling good self-care practices for other family members and caregivers. Most importantly, you are contributing to a healthier, more sustainable caregiving environment for your aging parents.

Interactive Element: Self-Care Techniques to Combat Stress and Burnout

Being a caregiver is rewarding but also extremely challenging. This section introduces various stress management techniques and self-care strategies you can incorporate into your daily routine to keep caregiver stress and burnout at bay.

Physical Health

- **Regular exercise:** Exercise is not only good for your physical health but also helps in stress management. Even a simple 20-30 minute walk daily can make a difference.

- **Get enough sleep:** While caregiving might demand that you keep irregular hours, sleep should never be compromised. According to the Cleveland Clinic (2019), poor sleep can significantly affect your emotional and physical well-being, impairing your decision-making skills and making you prone to mood swings. Aim for at least 7-8 hours of uninterrupted sleep per night to recharge both your body and mind.

- **Treat yourself to good, nutritious food:** Nutrition is the cornerstone of self-care. What you put into your body directly affects how you feel and function. A balanced diet rich in fruits, vegetables, lean proteins, and whole grains can provide sustained energy and better emotional balance.

- **Practice deep breathing exercises:** In moments of acute stress, deep breathing exercises can be lifesavers. The simple act of taking deep, controlled breaths can significantly lower stress levels almost instantaneously, providing a sense of calm and focus. Consider incorporating deep breathing into your daily routine to proactively manage stress.

- **Incorporate yoga or meditation into your nighttime routine:** Yoga and meditation have been shown to reduce stress hormones, enhance your mood, and improve your overall sense of well-being (Woodyard, 2011). Whether it's a simple 10-minute routine or a more intensive session, the key is consistency. Try incorporating these practices into your nightly routine to unwind and prepare your mind and body for restful sleep.

Emotional Well-Being

- **Join a support group:** The emotional toll of caregiving should never be underestimated. Joining a support group can provide a safe space to share experiences, gain insights, and feel understood. Harvard Health Blog highlights the benefits of these groups in providing emotional sustenance and practical caregiving tips (Wei, 2018).

- **Therapy or counseling:** Professional help can offer coping mechanisms to deal with the emotional and psychological stress of caregiving.

- **Practice self-compassion:** Taking care of someone else should not come at the cost of neglecting yourself. Remind yourself that you are also deserving of love and care. Self-compassion can be a powerful tool to counter stress and emotional exhaustion, helping you to be more patient and effective as a caregiver.

Mental Health

- **Mindfulness and meditation:** Even a few minutes of mindfulness or meditation can help refresh your mind, helping you tackle problems with a clearer perspective.

- **Time off:** No one can function without a break. If possible, arrange for alternate caregiving support so you can take some time off.

- **Make time for hobbies:** Your identity isn't solely tied to being a caregiver. Make time for activities that you love and that make you feel like yourself again. Whether it's painting, reading, or even a short walk in the park, these activities are not luxuries but necessities for your mental health.

Social Needs

- **Maintain other relationships:** Being a caregiver should not mean giving up on your other relationships. Make time for family and friends.

- **Engage in leisure activities:** Spend time doing things you love, whether it's reading, gardening, or any other hobby.

Educational Needs

- **Skills update:** Sometimes, caregiving can require specialized skills, like administering medication. Make sure you're updated on the latest best practices for caregiving.

Technological Help

- **App utilization:** There are several apps designed to help with stress management and meditation, but also apps specifically tailored for caregivers that help manage medication schedules, appointments, and more. Leverage technology to make your job easier.

- **Virtual socialization:** Sometimes leaving the house isn't an option. Use video calls to maintain social bonds or even have a virtual game night with friends.

Financial Self-Care

- **Budget planning:** The costs of caregiving can add up. Use budgeting tools or consult a financial advisor to ensure that you're not stretching yourself too thin. Some governments and organizations offer financial aid for caregivers, so it may be worthwhile to explore these options.

- **Insurance:** Look into insurance plans that might be beneficial for both you and the person you're caring for. This can help alleviate financial stress in case of medical emergencies.

Personal Development

- **Continued learning:** It might seem counterintuitive when you're already juggling so much, but sometimes engaging in a completely unrelated learning experience can be refreshing. Whether it's an online course, a cooking class, or a workshop, acquiring a new skill can be a form of self-care.

- **Career maintenance:** For those balancing caregiving with a professional life, don't neglect your own career development. See if your workplace offers flexible hours or consider remote work opportunities.

Environmental Tweaks

- **Aesthetics and atmosphere:** Never underestimate the power of a comfortable and pleasing environment. If you can, make small improvements to the space where you spend the most time. Scented candles, an ergonomic chair, or even a new paint color can make a big difference in your mood.

- **Noise control:** The constant beeping of medical devices or the sound of TV can get exhausting. High-quality noise-canceling headphones can offer an oasis of calm.

Advanced Medical Consultations

Genetic Counseling

If you're caring for a family member with a hereditary disease, consider genetic counseling for yourself. Understanding your own risks can be empowering and allow for proactive healthcare measures.

Alternative Therapies

Sometimes conventional medicine doesn't have all the answers. Therapies like acupuncture, chiropractic care, or even pet therapy have shown promise in reducing stress and improving well-being. Consult healthcare providers for advice tailored to your situation.

Self-care for caregivers extends far beyond the immediate needs of physical health and emotional well-being. By considering these additional avenues for self-care, you can create a more comprehensive plan that covers all facets of your life, making you a more effective and happier caregiver.

This discussion on self-care techniques sets the stage for the next chapter, which will focus on the second part of this topic—how external support and networking can further assist you in your caregiving journey. Remember, the most sustainable caregiving comes from a place of personal wellness. Take steps to ensure you're well-equipped, both emotionally and physically, to face the challenges caregiving may bring your way.

Chapter 7:

Self-Care for Caregivers, Part 2: Building a Support Network

This chapter will continue the topic of self-care for caregivers, again reiterating that the reader needs to take care of themselves physically, emotionally, mentally, and more. The previous chapter discussed self-care techniques. This chapter will discuss the importance of asking for help whenever possible and having an established support network.

> *When we seek for connection, we restore the world to wholeness. Our seemingly separate lives become meaningful as we discover how truly necessary we are to each other.* —Margaret J. Wheatley

The last chapter opened with the saying, "you cannot pour from an empty cup." The saying that best summarizes this chapter is, "no man is an island."

Caregiving and the Sandwich Generation

Some caregivers may care not only for an aging parent or partner but also for their own children. These caregivers are referred to as the "sandwich generation." About one in four caregivers fall into this category (Phillips, 2023). Sandwich generation caregivers may face additional emotional and financial challenges in caring for both children and parents. If you are a sandwich caregiver, consider how you might ask for help from family and friends. Others who are involved in caregiving may have suggestions to share.

Involving Family and Friends: Navigating the Complex Landscape of Shared Caregiving

One of the most effective strategies to create a sustainable caregiving experience and prevent burnout is to involve family and friends in the caregiving process. It's vital to remember that asking for and accepting help is not a sign of weakness but an act of resilience and practicality. When help is offered, graciously accept it; doing so enables a collective, more balanced approach to caregiving.

Leveraging Individual Strengths

Begin by conducting a personal skills inventory. What are your unique strengths, and how can they contribute to more effective caregiving? For example, if you have strong organizational skills, you may excel at coordinating medical appointments, tracking medication schedules, or maintaining accurate health records. On the other hand, if you have a financial background, your talents could be invaluable in managing insurance claims, paying bills, or deciphering medical invoices. If you're a natural leader, your skills could be well-suited for directing and managing a team of family and friend caregivers, ensuring that everyone works in harmony.

Identifying Limitations and Boundaries

Equally critical is understanding your limitations. Are you emotionally and mentally prepared for the complexities of role reversal, particularly if the person you're caring for is a parent? Can you handle challenges while maintaining respectful and assertive communication? Examine your own life circumstances as well and consider how they might be affected by your caregiving responsibilities. Be brutally honest about what you can realistically commit to. If being the primary caregiver is too much, perhaps you could serve as a respite caregiver, stepping in to offer temporary relief to the primary caregiver.

Clarifying Roles and Responsibilities

Once you've assessed strengths and limitations, the next step is to establish clear roles. This often involves organizing a family meeting, which should ideally include the person receiving care, if possible. The aim is to have a constructive conversation about current and future caregiving needs, away from the pressure of an immediate emergency. This proactive approach helps avoid confusion and tension later on. Many families benefit from designating a primary caregiver early in the process, even if the role is not immediately essential. This allows for a cohesive caregiving approach, where each person's contributions complement one another.

Involving Long-Distance Family Members

What about family members who live far away? Their contributions shouldn't be discounted. Even if they can't be physically present, they can offer various forms of support. This might include conducting online research about specific health conditions, identifying potential healthcare providers, or even exploring suitable assisted living facilities. Financial contributions or simply keeping the broader family network informed and emotionally supported can also be invaluable.

By approaching caregiving as a shared responsibility, you not only enrich the support structure around the person in need but also create a more manageable, less stressful experience for all involved.

Scheduling: The Key to Balanced Caregiving

The adage, "It takes a village," is particularly apt when it comes to caregiving. Even if you feel like you've got everything under control, reaching out to family and friends for assistance can bring immeasurable relief and create a more sustainable care routine. Establishing a caregiving schedule with willing participants isn't just about giving you a break; it's about ensuring that everyone involved maintains a healthy balance between caregiving responsibilities and their own lives.

By sharing duties, you lessen the risk of caregiver stress and burnout for everyone involved. When tasks and responsibilities are spread across a network, no single individual becomes overwhelmed, preserving the mental, emotional, and physical well-being of each caregiver. Whether it's organizing doctor's appointments, running errands, or just spending quality time with the parent, delegating tasks can make a world of difference.

If friends and family volunteer to be part of this rotational watch schedule, it's important to have open conversations about boundaries, much like the ones you've established for yourself. Discuss their comfort zones, limitations, and any other concerns that may come up in the caregiving process. By doing so, you can ensure that your support network is strong, cohesive, and, most importantly, enduring.

By integrating a rotational caregiving schedule into your life, you take an essential step toward long-term, balanced care for your aging parent, while also taking care of yourself and those who help you in this journey.

Creating and maintaining a network of assistance for elderly care comes with its unique set of challenges and considerations. Here are some additional issues for consideration:

Reliability and Consistency

Relying on a support network means you're depending on others to be there when you or your parent needs them. Sometimes people's circumstances change, making them unavailable. This inconsistency can make it difficult to ensure continuous, high-quality care.

Prevention: Create a "backup plan" for each member of your caregiving network. Make sure to have a short list of other willing helpers or professional services that can step in if someone becomes unavailable. Utilize digital calendars and scheduling apps to send reminders and updates to all involved to ensure that care is uninterrupted.

Coordination Complexity

As more people become involved in caregiving, coordinating schedules, responsibilities, and information sharing can become increasingly complicated. This often requires a designated person to act as a point of contact, further adding to their workload.

Prevention: Appoint a "care coordinator," someone responsible for managing the schedule and updating the team. Use project management software or apps designed for caregiving to streamline tasks, responsibilities, and updates. Periodic meetings can also help everyone stay aligned.

Differing Care Philosophies

Family members and friends may have varying opinions on how best to provide care. These differences can lead to tension or disagreements, especially when it comes to making important healthcare decisions.

Prevention: Establish a set of caregiving principles that everyone agrees upon and refer to these when conflicts arise. Medical professionals can often serve as neutral arbiters in these discussions. Being open to compromise is essential.

Financial Contributions

If the care network involves paid services, financial arrangements need to be transparent and agreed upon by all contributors. This can open a whole new area of discussion that may be uncomfortable for some family members.

Prevention: Have an open and candid discussion about finances early on and regularly update it. Document all agreed financial commitments and consult a financial advisor to oversee the arrangements if needed. Make all transactions as transparent as possible.

Privacy and Autonomy

Some seniors are uncomfortable with the idea of "outsiders" being heavily involved in their personal lives. It can be a challenge to balance the need for support with their desire for privacy and autonomy.

Prevention: Include the elderly individual in discussions about their care whenever possible. Be respectful of their wishes and clearly outline what each caregiver's role is to avoid "overstepping" into areas the senior is uncomfortable sharing.

Skills and Training

Not everyone in your network will have the necessary skills or understanding to care for an elderly individual. Training and orientation may be needed, especially for complex healthcare routines.

Prevention: Provide caregivers with proper training sessions or instructional guides for specific medical tasks. Engage healthcare professionals to provide basic caregiving training, and ensure all caregivers understand emergency procedures.

Legal and Ethical Concerns

When multiple people are involved in caregiving, issues such as consent, and liability can arise. Having legal documents that specify the rights and responsibilities of each caregiver can help but also adds another layer of complexity.

Prevention: Consult a lawyer to draft a caregiving agreement that clearly outlines the roles, responsibilities, and legal obligations of each caregiver. Make sure this is a living document that can be updated as situations change.

Communication Barriers

Keeping everyone in the loop is essential but not always straightforward. Whether due to geographic separation, or differences in communication styles, not everyone may be equally informed, leading to misunderstandings or errors in care.

Prevention: Regularly scheduled update meetings (in-person or virtual) can keep everyone informed. Use group messaging apps and email threads exclusively for caregiving updates and important announcements.

Emotional Dynamics

Family history and relationships can complicate caregiving. Old resentments or conflicts may resurface, affecting the quality of care and the emotional well-being of all involved.

Prevention: Address any interpersonal issues upfront to prevent them from affecting caregiving. Family or group therapy can provide a neutral space to air grievances and find constructive solutions.

Burnout Contagion

If one person in the network experiences stress or burnout, this can quickly affect others in the network, potentially compromising the care provided to the elderly parent.

Prevention: Monitor the emotional and physical well-being of all caregivers regularly. Encourage open dialogue about stress and burnout and have contingency plans in place (such as temporary professional caregiving support) to give anyone who feels overwhelmed a necessary break.

Socializing: A Win-Win for Caregivers and the Elderly

Caregiving isn't just about addressing physical needs; it's also about nurturing emotional well-being, both for you and the person you're caring for. One powerful way to uplift spirits all around is by encouraging socialization. Not only does socializing benefit the caregivers by giving them much-needed breaks, but it also profoundly impacts the seniors, elevating their mood and overall disposition.

Inviting your parent's friends for regular visits can be a game-changer for their emotional well-being. While you don't need to adhere to a strict schedule, facilitating such interactions—even if it's just a monthly brunch or dinner—can bring a refreshing change in your parent's life. Social engagement is crucial for seniors, as several studies have shown that it can lead to significant improvements in cognitive function and mental health (Carstensen & Hartel, 2006). For a deeper understanding of how socialization can help in avoiding isolation, check out articles by Caring Senior Service and Senior Lifestyle. These sources offer a comprehensive guide on how to encourage your older loved ones to become more socially active.

If your parents are physically able, why not consider signing them up for community events like "Senior's Night"? Not only are these events excellent opportunities for them to meet new people and engage in stimulating activities, but they also provide you with the chance to step back and take a breather from your caregiving responsibilities. The positive impact of such events on seniors' mental health has been corroborated by resources like Home Care Assistance Victoria and Home Care Assistance Oshkosh.

By incorporating social activities into your caregiving routine, you're not just giving yourself a reprieve. You're contributing to a richer, more fulfilling life for your parent. In the challenging world of caregiving, such win-win scenarios are golden opportunities that shouldn't be overlooked.

Utilizing Community Resources and Support Services: Expand Your Support Network Beyond Family and Friends

When the emotional, physical, and logistical aspects of caregiving become overwhelming, it's crucial to remember that you don't have to handle it alone. Various community resources and support services can greatly ease the load. Utilizing these services not only provides respite but also enhances the quality of care for your aging parent.

Community Resources and How They Can Help

First and foremost, take the time to familiarize yourself with the community resources available to you. There are senior centers, respite care services, adult day care facilities, and non-profit organizations dedicated to providing different forms of assistance to caregivers and the elderly. Websites like Caregiver.org and Maxim Healthcare offer comprehensive guides to these valuable resources, detailing how you can access and benefit from them.

Professional Assistance: More Than Just an Option

While family and friends can be an invaluable support network, hiring professional help is another feasible and highly effective solution. Options range from engaging a 24-hour nurse over the weekend to lighten your load, hiring a professional caregiver for a few hours daily, or even subscribing to a food delivery service that caters specifically to the nutritional needs of the elderly. By doing so, you free up time that can be better spent on activities that enrich your emotional connection with your aging parent, or simply taking a much-needed break to recharge.

The Role of Counseling in Caregiving

Lastly, counseling should not be overlooked as an additional resource for both caregivers and their parents. Therapy can offer a structured environment to address emotional and psychological challenges and develop coping strategies. The benefits of such intervention have been well documented in numerous sources, including Care.com, AgingCare.com, and the Alzheimer's Information Site. If you are skeptical about the time and effort required for counseling, rest assured that modern technology has made it more accessible than ever. Telehealth options are available, and some therapists even specialize in caregiver-specific issues.

By tapping into community resources and support services, including professional assistance and counseling, you bolster your own support network. This not only alleviates the burden you carry but also provides a holistic care environment for your aging parent. Remember, caregiving is a marathon, not a sprint; having the right resources and support can make all the difference.

Palliative Care and Assisted Living Centers

The topic of moving an elderly parent into an assisted living center can be emotionally charged and complex. As a caregiver, the decision about whether to transition your parent into such a facility can be heart-wrenching. Our purpose here is neither to endorse nor deter you from considering this option; rather, we present an unbiased overview of the pros and cons to help you make an informed choice.

Advantages and Disadvantages of Assisted Living Centers

Advantages

- **24/7 professional care:** A significant advantage of assisted living centers is their ability to provide continuous, professional medical supervision. For seniors with complex health needs, this level of attention can be difficult, if not impossible, to replicate in a home setting.

- **Social engagement:** Assisted living centers often feature a range of social activities—ranging from communal meals to organized games and outings—that help residents maintain emotional and mental well-being. This community aspect can significantly enhance the quality of life for seniors.

- **Enhanced safety measures:** These facilities are specifically designed with the safety of seniors in mind. From handrails in hallways to non-slip flooring and emergency alert systems, the built environment in assisted living centers is geared towards minimizing risks such as falls and other accidents.

Disadvantages

- **High costs:** Assisted living centers often require a considerable financial commitment. Depending on the facility and the range of services provided, the expenses can be substantial, necessitating either substantial out-of-pocket payments or comprehensive insurance coverage.

- **Emotional adjustment:** The transition from a familiar home environment to an assisted living center can be emotionally taxing for both the senior and their family members. Feelings of loss, changes in family dynamics, and adjustment to new routines are common challenges.

- **Variable quality of care:** The level of care and attention can vary significantly between different facilities. It's crucial to thoroughly research and, if possible, visit multiple centers before deciding to ensure that you're comfortable with the quality of care provided.

Advantages and Disadvantages of Providing Care at Home

Advantages

- **Familiar surroundings:** Perhaps the most compelling advantage of at-home care is the emotional comfort it offers your aging parent. The familiarity of their own home can be reassuring and offer a sense of continuity, which can be especially important for those suffering from cognitive issues like dementia.

- **Customized care:** Unlike institutional settings, where routines are typically fixed, at-home care provides the flexibility to tailor the care plan according to your parent's unique needs. Whether it's meal preferences or medication schedules, personalizing care becomes more manageable when it's provided at home.

- **Potential cost savings:** While at-home care is not necessarily inexpensive, it can offer some financial relief when compared to the often-hefty fees associated with high-quality aged homes. Depending on the level of care required, you may be able to manage with part-time professional assistance, further reducing costs.

Disadvantages

- **Limited professional supervision:** One of the challenges of opting for at-home care is the possibility of restricted access to round-the-clock professional medical care. While family members might take on the role of caregivers, the physical and emotional toll it takes can be significant, often leading to caregiver stress and burnout.

- **Risk of social isolation:** Unless proactively managed, taking care of your parent at home can potentially lead to isolation for both the caregiver and the care recipient. Without the social activities and peer interaction that a senior care facility often provides, an elderly individual may feel increasingly disconnected and lonely.

This chapter has underscored the importance of holistic self-care for caregivers. We've explored how setting boundaries, leaning on a reliable support network, and using community resources can be effective strategies for preventing caregiver stress and burnout. Whether you're contemplating sharing caregiving responsibilities with family members, utilizing community resources, or considering more formal care settings like palliative care or aged homes, remember—you don't have to go through this journey alone.

Resources

- National Respite Locator Service

- Well Spouse Association (800-838-0879)

- Caregiver Action Network (202-454-3970)

- Eldercare Locator (800-677-1116)

- Family Caregiver Ally (800-445-8106)

Chapter 8:

Celebrating Life and Coping with Loss

This chapter provides you with practical advice and emotional support to successfully manage caregiving during your loved one's twilight years. We will explore how you can make the most of the limited yet precious time you have with them, creating memories that will last a lifetime. Additionally, this chapter will offer guidance on how to emotionally prepare both yourself and your loved one for the inevitable transitions that lie ahead.

After my mom had a stroke, I cared for her 24/7 until she died in her own home two years later. It was the hardest thing I ever did in my life. But my mom and I had many moments of enjoyment, being together. We laughed. We cried. We were closer than ever before.
—Mary McKim, *The New York Times*

Quality Time and Meaningful Memories

The Gift of Presence

One of the most precious gifts caregiving can offer is the opportunity for quality time with your aging parent. With life's usual distractions set aside, the focus narrows down to human connections. The quality of these interactions can profoundly impact both your life and that of your elderly loved one. A study featured on Forbes suggests that simple, quality time is one of the leading factors contributing to the happiness of aging parents (Rosenblatt, 2021a).

The Ripple Effects of Emotional Health

Managing caregiver stress is crucial, not just for your well-being but to ensure that your interactions with your loved one are not tainted by negative emotions like frustration or anger. Remember, this is a crucial stage in your parent's life—a period when creating cherished memories should take precedence over tension and conflict. Research shows that quality time is more than just "feel-good" moments; it also has health benefits, including longevity (Park et al., 2014).

Creating Cherished Memories

The gravity of time's ticking clock should catalyze your desire to form lasting memories with your aging parent. Whether it's through simple conversations, shared laughter, or activities that bring joy, this is a period for cementing your relationship in meaningful ways. According to multiple sources, these shared experiences not only enrich your parent's life but also increase their overall well-being, potentially extending their lifespan (Thomas et al., 2017).

Practical Ways to Spend Quality Time

- **Learn their hobbies:** Engage in activities that your parents love. Whether it's gardening, knitting, or fishing, joining them in their hobbies can be an excellent way to bond.

- **Watch movies together:** Create a "movie night" tradition where you watch films that both of you enjoy. This can be an emotional release and a fun way to spend time together.

- **Cook together:** If your parent enjoys cooking, spend a day making a family recipe. This is not only a bonding experience but a great way to pass down family traditions.

- **Take a trip down memory lane:** Take time to look through old photos or home videos. This can be a meaningful way to relive happy memories and stimulate conversation.

- **Be a tourist in your own town:** Visit local attractions or museums that neither of you have been to. This adds a sense of adventure and new experiences to share.

By investing time and emotional energy, you can make this stage of life rich with meaningful interactions. Let this chapter serve as your guide in creating a nurturing environment where you can celebrate life while also preparing for the difficult but natural transitions that come with aging.

Coping With Grief and Loss

The Importance of Healthy Grieving

When the inevitable moment arrives and you face the loss of your loved one, it's crucial to allow yourself the space and time to grieve. Grieving is not a sign of weakness, but a natural and necessary emotional process. It helps you confront the reality of your loss and eventually find a way to live meaningfully without your loved one. According to experts, healthy grieving can lead to resolution and acceptance, instead of unresolved grief, which can be detrimental to your emotional health (Harvard Health, 2021).

Understanding Anticipatory Grief

In addition to the grief experienced after a loss, there's a distinct form of grief that often manifests while your loved one is still alive but terminally ill, known as "anticipatory grief." This type of grief often involves a combination of sadness, anxiety, guilt, and dread about what's coming. Though it shares many similarities with "regular" grief, it can be complicated by the fact that the person you're grieving for is still alive, adding an additional layer of emotional complexity.

The Five Stages of Grief

Understanding the grieving process can be instrumental in coming to terms with your feelings and in finding your path to healing. The concept of the "five stages of grief" was introduced by Swiss-American psychiatrist Elisabeth Kübler-Ross in her 1969 book, *On Death and Dying*. The model was initially developed based on observations of patients facing terminal illness, but it has been broadly applied to other types of grief and personal loss. The stages are not meant to be a rigid framework but rather a guide that can help people understand what they may be feeling after a loss. It's worth noting that not everyone will go through every stage, and some people may experience stages in a different order or cycle through some stages multiple times.

The five stages are as follows:

1. Denial

In this stage, the individual is struggling to believe the loss has occurred. They may feel numb or in shock, and the world might seem overwhelming or unreal. Denial serves as a coping mechanism to buffer the immediate shock of the loss. It helps us survive the grief event; we can only handle so much pain all at once.

2. Anger

As the denial fades, the reality and pain of the situation begin to set in, and many people feel angry. This anger can be directed at the deceased, oneself, survivors, doctors, or even fate. Anger gives structure to the nothingness of loss, providing some ground to stand on amidst upheaval. Though it may seem endless, the more truly and freely you can express it, the more quickly it will dissipate, allowing you to heal.

3. Bargaining

During this stage, the individual may make bargains with a higher power to reverse the loss, engaging in "what if" and "if only" statements. This is an attempt to regain control over the situation. People may ruminate on things they think they could have done differently to prevent death or loss. Bargaining is often accompanied by feelings of guilt.

4. Depression

After the individual has moved through denial, anger, and bargaining, the emotional despair of their loss sets in. This stage is characterized by feelings of emptiness, sadness, and regret. Depression after a loss is too often seen as unnatural or something to snap out of; however, like the other stages of grief, it is a natural and appropriate response to the situation.

5. Acceptance

The final stage of grief is acceptance, where the individual comes to terms with the loss and starts to look forward. Acceptance doesn't mean that the grieving person is perfectly fine or that they've forgotten their loved one, but rather that they've accepted this reality and are finding a way to live their life despite it. In this stage, the person may start to engage more with friends and family and take steps to move forward in life.

Understanding the five stages of grief can offer a structure in what may seem like a rollercoaster of emotions, helping individuals understand that what they are feeling is natural and that they are not alone. Recognizing where you are in these stages can serve as a roadmap for your emotional journey, helping you understand that your feelings are both normal and valid.

Tools and Techniques for Coping

- **Journaling:** Writing down your feelings and memories can provide an emotional outlet and can help you make sense of what you're going through.

- **Join a support group:** Grief can feel incredibly isolating. Talking with others who are going through similar experiences can offer emotional support and validation.

- **Physical activity:** Exercise may be the last thing on your mind, but physical activity releases endorphins, which naturally elevates your mood and helps you cope better with stress.

- **Seek professional help:** Sometimes, the weight of grief can be too heavy to bear alone. Therapists and counselors are trained to guide you through the grieving process.

- **Mindfulness and meditation:** Practices such as mindfulness and meditation can help you become aware of your thoughts, making it easier to control your emotional responses.

- **Create a memory book or memorial:** This can help you celebrate the life of the person you lost, making the grievous process also a celebration of a life well-lived.

- **Talk openly:** It can be therapeutic to speak openly about the person you have lost. Sharing memories can not only help you but also help others in their grieving process.

- **Art therapy:** Engaging in artistic activities like painting, sculpting, or even just doodling can be a form of emotional expression. Art therapy offers a way to visualize your feelings when words are not sufficient.

- **Music therapy:** Listening to or creating music can have a soothing effect. Some people find that certain types of music or songs offer comfort and a connection to their lost loved one.

- **Spiritual practices:** Whether it's prayer, attending religious services, or even just spending some quiet time in contemplation, many find solace in turning to their faith or spiritual beliefs during times of loss.

- **Pet therapy:** Animals offer unconditional love and are excellent companions when you're dealing with emotional pain. Even a brief interaction with an animal can lift your spirits.

- **Volunteer:** Helping others can sometimes provide a different perspective and can be uplifting. Whether it's in the memory of the lost one or simply a way to engage with the community, volunteering can be therapeutic.

- **Set up a ritual:** Creating a new ritual in memory of your loved one can be comforting. This could be lighting a candle every evening, visiting their grave or a place special to both of you on specific dates, or even watching a favorite movie of theirs annually.

- **Gardening:** For some, nurturing something else alive, like a garden, can be a healing practice. Planting a tree or a flower in memory of your loved one can be a long-lasting tribute.

- **Cooking or baking:** Making a favorite dish that your loved one enjoyed can be a form of therapy. The smells and tastes can evoke positive memories and feelings connected to the person you've lost.

- **Self-compassion:** Remember to be kind to yourself. Grieving is an emotionally taxing process, and it's okay not to be okay. Permit yourself the time and space to feel your emotions.

- **Financial planning:** While not emotionally therapeutic, getting your finances in order can alleviate some of the stress that comes with losing a family member, particularly if you are dealing with estate or funeral expenses. Consult with a financial advisor if needed.

- **Establish a living memorial or scholarship:** If appropriate, creating a memorial fund or scholarship in the name of your loved one can create a lasting legacy that benefits others, bringing a sense of meaning and positivity to a painful event.

- **Travel:** Sometimes a change of scenery can offer a new perspective and some emotional relief. It can also be an opportunity to visit places that had special meaning to the person you've lost.

Different methods work for different people, and it might take some time to discover which coping techniques are the most effective for you. Always remember, it's okay to seek professional guidance when you're navigating such complex emotions.

Understanding grief, its stages, and the tools to cope with it can be invaluable in navigating the complicated emotions surrounding the loss of a loved one. Your grief is a testament to your love, and it is that love that will see you through to finding a new normal—one where your loved one's memory is treasured but where you also find joy and meaning in the life you continue to live.

Interactive Element: Legacy Checklist

This section guides the reader through practical and heartwarming ways to celebrate their parents' legacy and honor their memory. These strategies will serve as a commemorative tribute that not only keeps their spirit alive but also provides a sense of closure and emotional enrichment for those left behind.

1. Create a Memory Book

Compile photographs, letters, recipes, or any other items that remind you of your parent. This memory book can be a tangible keepsake that you and other family members can turn to whenever you want to remember your loved one. It's also a wonderful way to introduce grandchildren or future generations to the ancestors they might not have had the chance to meet.

2. Host a Memorial Event

Organizing a memorial event like a "Celebration of Life" party allows family and friends to gather and share stories, memories, and emotions. This can include a slideshow of memorable moments, a playlist of their favorite songs, and even their favorite dishes. Refer to "Celebration of Life" for more details.

3. Plant a Tree or Garden

Nature has a way of healing us. Planting a tree or creating a garden in memory of your parent can be a long-lasting tribute to them. Each time you see it grow, you'll be reminded of their continual presence in your life.

4. Charitable Contributions

If your parent had a cause that was close to their heart, consider setting up or contributing to a charitable foundation in their name. It's a meaningful way to extend their influence and benevolence beyond their lifetime.

5. Memorial Scholarship

Create a scholarship fund in your parent's name to help students achieve their educational goals. This not only honors your parent's legacy but also invests in the future, something they were likely doing for you all their lives.

6. Annual Family Gathering

Designate a day each year to come together as a family to celebrate your parent's life. It could be on their birthday, the anniversary of their passing, or any other significant date. Use this time to share new and old stories, and maybe even add new items to the memory book.

7. Write and Share a Eulogy

Even if you're past the funeral stage, writing a eulogy—or a letter to your parent—can be a therapeutic exercise. Share it with family or keep it private, whichever feels right for you.

8. Personal Keepsakes

Convert a piece of your parent's clothing into a quilt or teddy bear. These items can be distributed among family members, offering a tangible piece of comfort and memory.

9. Online Memorial

Create a digital space where family and friends can share memories, pictures, and thoughts. Websites like CaringBridge offer platforms where you can do just that.

10. Cook a Family Recipe

Family recipes are more than just food; they're a legacy. Cooking a family recipe can invoke powerful memories and feelings. Make it a tradition to cook this recipe on special occasions or when you particularly miss them.

11. Light a Candle

Many cultures and religions use the act of lighting a candle as a symbolic gesture of remembrance. You could make it a regular practice, such as lighting a candle every Sunday, on special anniversaries, or during the holidays, to honor your parent's memory.

12. Memorial Artwork

Create or commission artwork that represents your parent's essence. It could be a painting, a sculpture, or even a piece of digital art. Display it in a special place in your home to serve as a daily reminder of their presence.

13. Memory Stones

Write your favorite memories or phrases that remind you of your parent on small stones. Place these in a garden, around a tree, or in a special container. These can serve as small yet meaningful tokens that you can pick up and hold whenever you're thinking of them.

14. Release of Balloons or Lanterns

On special occasions, some people find solace in releasing balloons or lanterns with messages written on them to the sky. This can be a liberating and therapeutic way to send your thoughts or prayers up to your loved one.

15. Create a Playlist

Music often evokes powerful emotions and memories. Create a playlist of songs that remind you of your parent or that include their favorite tunes. Play it during moments when you want to feel connected to them.

16. Remembrance Jewelry

You can have custom jewelry made that incorporates something belonging to your parent, like a small photograph, a lock of hair, or even some of their ashes. Wearing it can keep them close to your heart, both metaphorically and literally.

17. Virtual Memorial Service

For family members and friends who can't be there physically, consider organizing a virtual memorial service. This will allow everyone to partake in the celebration of your parent's life, regardless of where they are in the world.

18. Craft Time with Grandkids

If there are grandchildren, consider doing crafts that help them remember their grandparent. This could be as simple as making a scrapbook together or building a small birdhouse that reminds you of your parent.

19. Documentary or Video Tribute

Compile home videos, photos, and interviews with family members and friends to create a video tribute to your parent. This could be shared online or played during family gatherings.

20. Storytime

If your parent was a storyteller or had some memorable stories that you associate with them, consider writing these down and sharing them with others. Whether it's children, younger family members, or even a wider audience through a blog or social media, sharing these stories keeps their spirit alive through the art of storytelling.

Each of these activities offers a unique way to remember, celebrate, and even grieve the loss of your parent. The key is to choose the ones that resonate most with you and the relationship you had with your loved one. You'll be paying a lasting tribute to your parents while also finding personal comfort and emotional healing.

Conclusion

As you close the final chapter of this book, it's essential to reflect on the journey we've taken together. The road to understanding how to care for an aging parent, how to cherish the time we have left with them, and how to handle the emotionally dense terrain of grief and loss, is far from easy. Yet, it's a road filled with invaluable lessons, moments of undeniable joy, and the kind of emotional growth that transforms us in ways we could never anticipate.

The crux of this book lies in its commitment to help you make the most of an emotionally demanding, often overwhelming, period in both your life and that of your aging parent. From understanding the healthcare system to managing finances to spending quality time and coping with loss, the tools and advice outlined are designed to provide you with the knowledge you need to successfully move through these complex stages with a measure of grace, resilience, and emotional fortitude.

Let's not forget Mary McKim's journey that we began this chapter with. She looked after her mom 24/7 after a debilitating stroke. It was undeniably tough, but it was also rich with moments of love, closeness, and genuine happiness. Through all the hardship, she discovered a new layer of relationship with her mother. It's a testament to what can be achieved when you approach this challenging period not just as a time of impending loss, but as an opportunity for unprecedented connection.

So, what's next?

Your First Call-to-Action

Armed with the tools and insights from this book, you are no longer a wanderer but a warrior, prepared to confront the physical, emotional, and mental challenges of caring for an elderly parent. Utilize the resources and methods discussed to make this stage as enriching as possible for both you and your parent.

Your Second Call-to-Action

The network of support available to you is vast and rich with potential. From professionals in healthcare to online support groups, you're not alone on this journey. Use these resources to replace fear and frustration with grace and resilience.

As we come to the end, if this book has provided you with the comfort, understanding, or guidance you were seeking, please consider leaving a review. Your thoughts will not only assist us in honing this resource but will also aid others who find themselves on a similar path.

Thank you for allowing me to be a part of your journey. May it be a path that, while challenging, is strewn with moments of joy, love, and profound connection.

References

ABA. (2013). *Power of Attorney*. American Bar Association. https://www.americanbar.org/groups/real_property_tr ust_estate/resources/estate_planning/power_of_attorn ey/

AgingCare. (2023). *The Importance of Counseling for Caregivers*. AgingCare. https://www.agingcare.com/articles/counseling-for-caregiver-burnout-126208.htm

Alzheimer's Association. (2023). *What Is Alzheimer's?* Alzheimer's Association. https://www.alz.org/alzheimers-dementia/what-is-alzheimers

American Psychological Association. (2023). *American Psychological Association*. Apa.org. https://www.apa.org/

Andrews, M. (2020, December 4). *Think Your Health Care Is Covered? Beware of the "Junk" Insurance Plan*. KFF Health News. https://kffhealthnews.org/news/junk-insurance-plans-health-consumers-beware/

APA. (2011). *Our Health at Risk*. American Psychological Association.https://www.apa.org/news/press/releases /stress/2011/final-2011.pdf

APA. (2020, January 1). *Grief: Coping with the loss of your loved one*. American Psychological Association. https://www.apa.org/topics/families/grief

APA. (2021, September). *Older adults' health and age-related changes.* American Psychological Association. https://www.apa.org/pi/aging/resources/guides/older

Ardron, B. (2023, July 25). *How to Talk To Your Parents About Funeral and Cemetery Pre-Planning.* LinkedIn. https://www.linkedin.com/pulse/how-talk-your-parents-funeral-cemetery-pre-planning-brenna-ardron

Arwin. (n.d.). *Why am I Getting Burnt Out Taking Care of My Parents?.* Ohana. https://www.ohanaisfamily.com/blog/why-am-i-getting-burnt-out-taking-care-of-my-parents

ASC. (2017, August 29). *The Challenges Facing a Family Caregiver.* American Senior Communities. https://www.asccare.com/the-challenges-facing-a-family-caregiver/

Ashford, K. (2021, November 18). *How to Balance Work and Caregiving.* WebMD. https://www.webmd.com/healthy-aging/caregiver-balance-work

Austrew, A. (2022, March 18). *How to help older adults navigate the difficult emotional effects of aging.* Care.com. https://www.care.com/c/helping-seniors-navigate-emotional-effects-of-aging/

Bean, M. (2023, May 2). *Power of Attorney for Elderly Parents.* A Place for Mom. https://www.aplaceformom.com/caregiver-resources/articles/power-of-attorney-guide#why-aging-parents-need-a-power-of-attorney

Berman, C. (2016, March 4). *What Aging Parents Want From Their Adult Children*. The Atlantic. https://www.theatlantic.com/health/archive/2016/03/when-youre-the-aging-parent/472290/

Bernard, T. S. (2013, May 24). The Talk You Didn't Have With Your Parents Could Cost You. *The New York Times*. https://www.nytimes.com/2013/05/25/your-money/aging-parents-and-children-should-talk-about-finances.html

Better Health. (2015). *Aging - muscles bones and joints*. Better Health Channel. https://www.betterhealth.vic.gov.au/health/conditions andtreatments/ageing-muscles-bones-and-joints

Bieber, C. (2021, October 14). *Why Retirees Still Need an Emergency Fund*. The Motley Fool. https://www.fool.com/investing/2021/10/14/why-retirees-still-need-an-emergency-fund/

Bolen, J. (2022, November 4). *3 Reasons Healthcare Navigation is Essential for Your Patients*. IBizz Web. https://ibizzweb.com/3-reasons-healthcare-navigation-is-essential-for-your-patients/

Bond, C. (2022, July 29). *How to Legally Take Over Your Parent's Finances*. The Balance. https://www.thebalancemoney.com/taking-over-elderly-parents-finances-legally-6361456#toc-when-to-take-over-your-parents-finances

Bradley Bursack, C. (2023). *How "Role Reversal" and Other Caregiving Catchphrases Skew Your Thoughts*. AgingCare.

https://www.agingcare.com/articles/dont-let-role-reversal-skew-your-thinking-113670.htm

Brock, C. (2020, June 24). *Power of Attorney Guide: What Is It and How to Get It for Parents.* Harbor Life Settlements. https://www.harborlifesettlements.com/how-get-power-of-attorney-elderly-parents/

Bumgardner, S. (2023, May 26). *What you should know about managing aging parents' finances.* The News Herald. https://www.thenewsherald.com/2023/05/26/what-you-should-know-about-managing-aging-parents-finances/

Butler, C. (2021, August 24). *12 Ways to Honor the Legacy of a Loved One and Get Closure.* Power of Positivity: Positive Thinking & Attitude. https://www.powerofpositivity.com/legacy-loss-loved-one/

Caregivers and Families. (2020, February 10). *9 Warning Signs of Deteriorating Health in Aging Adults.* Exceptional Living Centers. https://exceptionallivingcenters.com/9-warning-signs-of-deteriorating-health-in-aging-adults/

Carelink. (2020, May 21). *Tips for sharing the caregiver role with siblings.* CareLink. https://www.carelink.org/tips-for-sharing-the-caregiver-role-with-siblings/

CaringBridge. (2022, November 18). *9 Celebration of Life Ideas to Honor Your Loved One.* CaringBridge. https://www.caringbridge.org/resources/celebration-of-life-ideas/

CaringInfo. (2023). *Caregiving Resources & Links for Support.* CaringInfo. https://www.caringinfo.org/planning/caregiving/careg iving-resources

Carr, D. (2022, January 10). *End-of-life conversations can be hard, but your loved ones will thank you.* The Conversation. https://theconversation.com/end-of-life-conversations-can-be-hard-but-your-loved-ones-will-thank-you-173614

Carstensen, L. L., & Hartel, C. R. (2006). *Social Engagement and Cognition.* National Library of Medicine; National Academies Press (US). https://www.ncbi.nlm.nih.gov/books/NBK83766/

CDC. (2019, April 24). *Centers for Disease Control and Prevention.* Centers for Disease Control and Prevention. https://www.cdc.gov/index.htm

CDC. (2021, April 29). *Loneliness and Social Isolation Linked to Serious Health Conditions.* Center for Disease Control and Prevention. https://www.cdc.gov/aging/publications/features/lon ely-older-adults.html

Cemental, M. (2021). *How to Celebrate Your Aging Parents.* Caring Senior Service. https://www.caringseniorservice.com/blog/how-to-celebrate-your-aging-parents

Cemental, R. (2021). *Ways to Help Seniors Socialize and Avoid Isolation.* Caring Senior Service.

https://www.caringseniorservice.com/blog/ways-to-help-seniors-avoid-isolation

Chand, S., & Arif, H. (2023, July 17). *Depression*. PubMed; StatPearls Publishing. https://www.ncbi.nlm.nih.gov/books/NBK430847/

Charles, S. T., & Carstensen, L. L. (2010, January 10). Social and Emotional Aging. *Annual Review of Psychology*, *61*(1), 383–409. https://doi.org/10.1146/annurev.psych.093008.100448

Chatzky, J. (2017, April 30). *How to manage the legal side of taking care of aging parents*. NBC News. https://www.nbcnews.com/business/personal-finance/taking-care-aging-parents-legal-financial-details-you-need-know-n752486

Cleveland Clinic. (2019, January 13). *Caregiver Burnout*. Cleveland Clinic. https://my.clevelandclinic.org/health/diseases/9225-caregiver-burnout

Cogan, M. (2022, September 30). *End-of-life planning with loved ones can be hard. Here's where to start*. Vox. https://www.vox.com/even-better/23378958/end-of-life-planning-elders-parents-grandparents-loved-ones

Colby. (2018, January 4). *Coping with Role Reversal*. The Lisa Vogel Agency. https://lisavogelagency.com/coping-role-reversal/

Companion for Seniors. (2018, November 28). *How to Handle a Role Reversal With Your Aging Parent*. Companions for Seniors.

https://companionsforseniors.com/2018/11/role-reversal-aging-parent/

Cooper, M. (2023, March 10). *10+ Fun Things to Do With Elderly Parents You'll Both Enjoy.* LoveToKnow. https://www.lovetoknow.com/life/aging/things-do-elderly-parents

Daily Beacon. (2021, March 23). *Pros And Cons Of Retirement Village Living.* The Daily Beacon. https://www.dailybeacon.com.au/pros-and-cons-of-retirement-village-living/

Daily Caring. (2023). *Helping Aging Parents With Finances: 5 Ways to Reduce Resistance.* DailyCaring. https://dailycaring.com/5-keys-to-helping-aging-parents-with-finances/

Dalton, B. (2021, December 21). *Plan For Your Earthly Departure.* Crow's Feet. https://medium.com/crows-feet/plan-for-your-earthly-departure-60aeae2e35ba

Dastagir, A. E. (2021, July 8). *Furious at your parents for aging? You're not alone.* USA Today. https://www.usatoday.com/story/life/health-wellness/2021/07/08/children-caregiving-aging-parents-feel-anger-stress-frustration/7901360002/

Davis, T. (2023, March 10). *Navigating Family Dynamics in Caregiving.* Commonwealth Senior Living. https://www.commonwealthsl.com/navigating-family-dynamics-in-caregiving/

Dev, H. (2020, March 6). *How Can I Share My Caregiving Responsibilities with Others?.* Home Care Assistance.

https://www.homecareassistancewinnipeg.ca/how-family-caregivers-can-share-duties-with-others/

Dimery, P. (2021, September 4). *The importance of quality time.* Boundless. https://www.boundless.co.uk/be-inspired/wellbeing/how-to-spend-more-quality-time-with-your-family

Donohue, M. (2021, July 2). *5 of the Most Common Causes of Mood Swings in Elderly Women.* Blue Moon Senior Counseling. https://bluemoonseniorcounseling.com/5-causes-of-mood-swings-in-elderly-women/

Drake, K. (2021, July 1). *Relationship changes: Why they happen and what to do.* Psych Central. https://psychcentral.com/blog/change-in-relationships-what-to-do-when-your-partner-changes

Ducher & Zatkowsky. (2019, May 21). *Why Seniors Should Engage in Estate Planning.* Rochester Elder Law. https://www.rochesterelderlaw.com/why-seniors-should-engage-in-estate-planning

Eisenberg, R. (2019, August 11). *Balancing Your Career And Your Aging Parents.* Forbes. https://www.forbes.com/sites/nextavenue/2019/08/11/balancing-your-career-and-your-aging-parents/?sh=3cbb1eab3a59

Eldridge, L. (2013, January 14). *Coping With Anticipatory Grief.* Verywell Health. https://www.verywellhealth.com/coping-with-anticipatory-grief-2248856

Esposito , L., & Howley, E. K. (2022, December 16). *How to Coordinate Care for Your Elderly Parents With Siblings.* US News. https://health.usnews.com/senior-care/caregiving/articles/coordinate-aging-parents-with-siblings

Everyday Health. (2023). *10 Health Conditions to Watch for as You Age.* Everyday Health. https://www.everydayhealth.com/senior-health-photos/conditions-to-watch-for.aspx

Family Caregiver Alliance. (2023). *Caregiving at Home: A Guide to Community Resources.* Family Caregiver Alliance. https://www.caregiver.org/resource/caregiving-home-guide-community-resources/

Family Caregiver Alliance. (2023). *Taking Care of YOU: Self-Care for Family Caregivers.* Family Caregiver Alliance. https://www.caregiver.org/resource/taking-care-you-self-care-family-caregivers/

Family Caregivers Online. (2022, March). *Behavior and Emotions of Aging.* Family Caregivers Online. https://familycaregiversonline.net/caregiver-education/behavior-and-emotions-of-aging/

Ferrucci, L., Cooper, R., Shardell, M., Simonsick, E. M., Schrack, J. A., & Kuh, D. (2016, March 14). Age-Related Change in Mobility: Perspectives From Life Course Epidemiology and Geroscience. *The Journals of Gerontology Series A: Biological Sciences and Medical Sciences, 71*(9), 1184–1194. https://doi.org/10.1093/gerona/glw043

First in Care. (2020, December 7). *Role Reversal in Caregiving.* First in Care. https://www.firstincare.com/aging-in-place-as-a-family/role-reversal-in-caregiving/

Fisher, M. (2023). *Causes and Symptoms of Caregiver Burnout.* Hopkins Medicine. https://www.hopkinsmedicine.org/about/community_health/johns-hopkins-bayview/services/called_to_care/causes_symptoms_caregiver_burnout.html

Fiske, A., Wetherell, J. L., & Gatz, M. (2009, April 27). Depression in Older Adults. *Annual Review of Clinical Psychology,* *5*(1), 363–389. https://doi.org/10.1146/annurev.clinpsy.032408.153621

Freedman, D. (2023, September 28). *6 Reasons You Need an Emergency Fund in Retirement.* Take Care. https://getcarefull.com/articles/6-reasons-you-need-an-emergency-fund-in-retirement

Freeman, A. (2023, June 9). *12 Tips for Balancing Your Life as a Family Caregiver.* LoveToKnow. https://www.lovetoknow.com/life/aging/balance-life-as-family-caregiver

Frontiers. (2019). *Article.* Frontiers. https://www.frontiersin.org/articles/

Galindo, M. (2023, February 21). *5 Tips for Navigating The U.S. Healthcare System.* Acensa Health. https://acensahealth.com/2023/02/21/5-tips-for-navigating-the-healthcare-system/

Gastfriend, J. (2018, August 29). *When Siblings Share The Caregiving For An Aging Parent, Will It Be Welfare Or Warfare?* Forbes. https://www.forbes.com/sites/jodygastfriend/2018/0 8/29/15siblings-caring-for-parents/?sh=cd7537375916

Gillette , H., & Casabianca, S. S. (2021, July 21). *6 Coping Skills For Managing Grief and Loss.* Psych Central. https://psychcentral.com/health/coping-skills-for-grief#coping-skills-vs-self-care

Godman, H. (2022, February 28). *Taking an aging parent to the doctor? 10 helpful tips.* Harvard Health. https://www.health.harvard.edu/blog/taking-an-aging-parent-to-the-doctor-10-helpful-tips-202202282696

Gordon, D. (2015, August). *How to Start Talking About End-of-Life Care.* Brain & Life. https://www.brainandlife.org/articles/people-who-discuss-their-end-of-life-wishes-are-less

Graham, J. (2023a, March 31). Fatigue is common among older people. Finding its cause is important. *Washington Post.* https://www.washingtonpost.com/health/2023/03/31/fatigue-older-adults-causes/

Graham, J. (2023b, May 17). *When older parents resist help or advice, use these tips to cope.* CNN. https://edition.cnn.com/2023/05/17/health/aging-parents-resisting-help-kff-partner-wellness/index.html

Gregory, M. (2023, January 10). *Helpful Resources for Family Caregivers.* Maxim Healthcare Services.

https://www.maximhealthcare.com/healthcare-blog/resources-for-family-caregivers/

Griese, L., Berens, E.-M., Nowak, P., Pelikan, J. M., & Schaeffer, D. (2020, August 8). Challenges in Navigating the Health Care System: Development of an Instrument Measuring Navigation Health Literacy. *International Journal of Environmental Research and Public Health, 17*(16). https://doi.org/10.3390/ijerph17165731

Grossman, J. (2020, September 21). *Pros and Cons of Putting Elderly Parents in Nursing Homes.* Commonwise Home Care. https://www.commonwisecare.com/pros-and-cons-of-putting-elderly-parents-in-nursing-homes/

Guardian. (2023). *How to Talk to Aging Parents About Finances.* Guardian Life. https://www.guardianlife.com/retirement/aging-parents-finances

Guthrie, P. (2015, May 2). *How To Cope When You Reverse Roles With Your Aging Parents.* HuffPost. https://www.huffpost.com/entry/aging-parents_b_7133388

Harvard Health. (2021, February 15). *How to overcome grief's health-damaging effects.* Harvard Health Publishing. https://www.health.harvard.edu/mind-and-mood/how-to-overcome-griefs-health-damaging-effects

Hasson, J. (2022, January 21). *A Legal Checklist for Family Caregivers.* AARP.

https://www.aarp.org/caregiving/financial-legal/info-2020/caregivers-legal-checklist.html

Health Care Assistance. (2022, August 18). *Why Is Socialization Essential for Elderly People?* Home Care Assistance. https://www.homecareassistanceoshkosh.com/why-do-seniors-need-to-socialize/

HealthDay News. (2022, April 11). *Caring For Yourself While Caregiving For Aging Parents.* Franciscan Health Alliance. https://www.franciscanhealth.org/community/blog/caring-for-aging-parents-and-self

Health Essentials. (2023, February 24). *Caregivers Need Self-Care, Too.* Cleveland Clinic. https://health.clevelandclinic.org/self-care-for-caregivers/

Healthline. (2018, November 26). *How to Care for Yourself When You Have Caregiver Burnout.* Healthline. https://www.healthline.com/health/health-caregiver-burnout

Heid, M. (2023, March 17). *How to Cope With Grief.* Everyday Health. https://www.everydayhealth.com/emotional-health/grief/healthy-grieving/

Henry Ford Health. (2023, January 30). *How To Maintain Muscle Mass As You Age.* Henry Ford Health. https://www.henryford.com/blog/2023/01/how-to-maintain-muscle-mass-as-you-age

Hicks, P. (n.d.-a). *What is a Formal Will? What You Need to Know.* Trust & Will. https://trustandwill.com/learn/formal-will

Hicks, P. (n.d.-b). *What Is a Will: Your Guide to Last Will &* *Testaments.* Trust & Will. https://trustandwill.com/learn/what-is-a-will

Highgate Senior Living. (n.d.). *5 Tips for Setting Realistic Boundaries as a Family Caregiver.* Highgate Senior Living. https://blog.highgateseniorliving.com/5-tips-for-setting-realistic-boundaries-and-expectations-as-a-family-caregiver

Holland, K. (2018, September 25). *Stages of Grief: General Patterns for Breakups, Divorce, Loss, More.* Healthline. https://www.healthline.com/health/stages-of-grief

Home Care Assistance. (2020, August 6). *How to Balance Caregiving with Other Family Roles.* Home Care Assistance. https://www.homecareassistancehuntsville.com/balancing-family-roles-with-caring-for-an-older-parent/

Home Care Assistance Tampa Bay. (2020, May 5). *6 Ways Aging Affects Emotions.* Home Care Assistance Tampa Bay. https://www.homecareassistancetampabay.com/emotional-impacts-of-growing-older/

Huddleston, C. (2019, August 21). *10 Ways to Talk to Your Aging Parents About Their Finances.* Kiplinger. https://www.kiplinger.com/slideshow/retirement/t013-s001-talk-to-your-aging-parents-about-their-finances/index.html

Jaga Me. (2022). *Child to Caregiver: What can you do about role reversal?* The Care Issue. https://jaga-me.com/thecareissue/role-reversal/

Jaul, E., & Barron, J. (2017, December 11). Age-Related Diseases and Clinical and Public Health Implications for the 85 Years Old and Over Population. *Frontiers in Public Health, 5*(335). https://doi.org/10.3389/fpubh.2017.00335

Jeurkar, R. (2017, September 18). *When the roles are reversed: Caring for your elderly parents.* White Swan Foundation. https://www.whiteswanfoundation.org/caregiving/wh en-the-roles-are-reversed-caring-for-your-elderly-parents

John Hopkins. (2023). *Johns Hopkins Medicine: An Ongoing Commitment to Community.* Hopkins Medicine. https://www.hopkinsmedicine.org/about/community_ health/johns-hopkins-

John Hopkins. (n.d.-a). *Tough (But Important) Conversations.* Hopkins Medicine. https://www.hopkinsmedicine.org/health/wellness-and-prevention/tough-but-important-conversations

John Hopkins. (n.d.-b). *Advance Directives.* Hopkins Medicine. https://www.hopkinsmedicine.org/patient-care/patients-visitors/advance-directives

Juliano, S. (2017, February 20). *Pros and Cons of Keeping Your Aging Loved One at Home.* Presbyterian Senior Living. https://www.presbyterianseniorliving.org/blog/pros-cons-keeping-senior-home

Kane, E. C. (2023, July 11). *Pros And Cons Of Aging In Place.* Senior Safety Advice.

https://seniorsafetyadvice.com/pros-and-cons-of-aging-in-place/

Kelly, K. (2014, October 23). *How to balance your career with the needs of an aging family member.* PBS NewsHour. https://www.pbs.org/newshour/health/juggling-work-care-aging-loved-ones

Kernisan, L. (2019, August 24). *6 Ways that Thinking Changes with Aging (& What to Do About This).* Better Health While Aging. https://betterhealthwhileaging.net/how-brain-function-changes-with-normal-cognitive-aging/

Kernisan, L. (2019, September 20). *9 Types of Issues to Address When Helping Older Parents.* Better Health While Aging. https://betterhealthwhileaging.net/what-to-address-when-helping-older-parents/

Kiau, H. B. (2016, August 12). *Emotional Changes Among Older Person.* MyHealth. http://www.myhealth.gov.my/en/types-emotional-changes-among-older-person/

Knueven, L. (2020, February 26). *How to talk with your parents about their estate plan, even if they don't want to.* Business Insider. https://www.businessinsider.com/personal-finance/parents-estate-plan-how-to-talk-about

Konstanzer, C. (2023, May 1). *Caring for Aging Loved Ones.* Winter Growth. https://www.wintergrowthinc.org/caring-for-aging-loved-ones/

Lake, R. (2021, December 12). *How Much Money Should Retirees Have in an Emergency Fund?* The Balance.

https://www.thebalancemoney.com/how-much-emergency-savings-do-retirees-need-4582473

Lamb, E. (2022, May 26). *All Too Common Challenges In Caring For The Elderly*. My Place Health Care. https://myplacehealthcare.com/all-too-common-challenges-in-caring-for-the-elderly/

Lauria, P. (2022, August 15). *Estate Planning for Aging Parents: It's Never Too Late*. The Balance. https://www.thebalancemoney.com/estate-planning-for-aging-parents-6455494

Lawrence, B. (2014, November 28). *A sibling's guide to caring for aging parents*. PBS NewsHour. https://www.pbs.org/newshour/health/youre-sharing-care-aging-parents

Lee, K. (2019, August 26). *Aging Parents: How to Spot Potential Health Problems*. Everyday Health. https://www.everydayhealth.com/family-health/aging-parents.aspx

Lee, M. S. (2022, February 18). *I'm a financial planner, and I tell anyone caring for aging parents to take 3 steps before it's too late*. Business Insider. https://www.businessinsider.com/personal-finance/things-should-do-providing-care-for-elderly-parents-2022-2

Lerner, J. S., Li, Y., Valdesolo, P., & Kassam, K. S. (2015, January). Emotion and decision making. *Annual Review of Psychology, 66*(1), 799–823.

https://doi.org/10.1146/annurev-psych-010213-115043

Lifestyle. (2021a, May 7). *10 Fun Activities You Can Do With Elderly Parents.* Times Union. https://blog.timesunion.com/lifestyle/10-fun-activities-you-can-do-with-elderly-parents/1430/

Lower Cape Fear LifeCare. (2018, August 17). *5 Useful Tools to Capture Your Parent's Legacy & Honor Their Favorites.* Lower Cape Fear LifeCare. https://lifecare.org/news-events/5-ways-honor-parents-legacy/

Maertz, K. (2021, June 8). *Strategies to Cope with Grief.* UNICEF. https://www.unicef.org/armenia/en/stories/strategies-cope-grief

Mancini, J. A., & Blieszner, R. (1989, May). Aging Parents and Adult Children: Research Themes in Intergenerational Relations. *Journal of Marriage and the Family*, 51(2), 275. https://doi.org/10.2307/352492

Mariano, L. (2019, December 20). *6 Strategies for Engaging the Elderly in Social Activities.* Home Care Assistance Victoria. https://homecareassistancevictoria.ca/how-can-i-encourage-my-older-loved-one-to-get-socially-active/

Martin, L. (2022, February 28). *Caregiver burnout: Symptoms, prevention, and more.* Medical News Today. https://www.medicalnewstoday.com/articles/caregiver-burnout

Mayo Clinic. (2023, September 20). *Aging: What to expect.* Mayo
Clinic. https://www.mayoclinic.org/healthy-
lifestyle/healthy-aging/in-depth/aging/art-20046070

Mayo Clinic Staff. (2023, August 9). *Practical solutions for caregiver
stress.* Mayo Clinic.
https://www.mayoclinic.org/healthy-lifestyle/stress-
management/in-depth/caregiver-stress/art-20044784

McDuffey, T. (2023, April 15). *Estate Planning For Elderly Parents
(Complete Guide).* Trustworthy.
https://www.trustworthy.com/blog/estate-planning-
for-elderly-parents

Mesroblan, C. (2022, January 31). *Health Literacy: What Is It and
Why Is It Important?* Rasmussen University.
https://www.rasmussen.edu/degrees/health-
sciences/blog/importance-of-health-literacy/

Mihaly, J. (2019, April 22). *7 Hard But Necessary Conversations to
Have With Your Aging Parents.* Fatherly.
https://www.fatherly.com/life/conversations-to-have-
with-aging-parents

Miller, K. F. (2019, August 20). *Funeral Planning With My Family.*
Human Parts.
https://humanparts.medium.com/funeral-planning-
with-my-family-1d3ca0f31387

Mitchell, C. G. (2022, March 28). *It Depends - What is an informal
Will?* Lexology.
https://www.lexology.com/library/detail.aspx?g=8f144
395-4ae4-4768-ae41-f64b673c8707

Mittelman, M. (2009, October 8). *Alzheimer's Caregivers Stay Healthier with Counseling.* Fisher Center for Alzheimer's Research Foundation. https://www.alzinfo.org/articles/alzheimers-caregivers-stay-healthier-with-counseling/

MoneyGeek. (2021, July 20). *Managing Elderly Parents' Finances.* MoneyGeek.com. https://www.moneygeek.com/seniors/resources/managing-elderly-parents-finances/

Murman, D. L. (2015). The Impact of Age on Cognition. *Seminars in Hearing, 36*(03), 111–121. https://doi.org/10.1055/s-0035-1555115

Najjar, M. (2023, January 13). *The One Thing You Can Give Your Parents To Help Them Live Longer, Happier Lives.* YourTango. https://www.yourtango.com/family/spending-time-with-aging-parents-helps-them-live-longer

Nason, D. (2021, November 30). *Waiting to talk finance with an aging parent in cognitive decline is a mistake, experts say.* CNBC. https://www.cnbc.com/2021/11/30/here-are-financial-moves-to-make-when-elderly-parents-start-to-decline.html

Nelson, C. (2023, February 19). *Role reversals: 5 things to consider.* Caregiver Solutions Magazine. https://caregiversolutions.ca/caregiving/role-reversals-5-things-to-consider/

NerdWallet. (2022, January 16). *How to help your parents navigate health care in retirement.* Cleveland.

https://www.cleveland.com/news/2022/01/how-to-help-your-parents-navigate-health-care-in-retirement.html

Next Avenue. (2022, June 30). *Tips For Older Adults Navigating The Health Care System*. Forbes. https://www.forbes.com/sites/nextavenue/2022/06/30/tips-for-older-adults-navigating-the-health-care-system/?sh=6ccc95db2537

NIA. (2017, May 9). *How to Share Caregiving Responsibilities with Family Members*. National Institute on Aging. https://www.nia.nih.gov/health/how-share-caregiving-responsibilities-family-members

NIA. (2020). *10 Myths About Aging*. National Institute on Aging. https://www.nia.nih.gov/health/10-myths-about-aging

NIA. (2022, October 31). *Advance Care Planning: Advance Directives for Health Care*. National Institute on Aging. https://www.nia.nih.gov/health/advance-care-planning-advance-directives-health-care#without

NIH. (2017, September 28). *Coping With Grief*. News in Health. https://newsinhealth.nih.gov/2017/10/coping-grief

Off The Mrkt. (2022, October 25). *Caring For Aging Parents: Common Challenges And How To Avoid Them*. Off the MRKT. https://www.offthemrkt.com/lifestyle/caring-for-aging-parents-common-challenges-and-how-to-avoid-them

Ong, V. (n.d.). *Family Caregiver Alliance*. Caregiver. https://www.caregiver.org/resource/parenting-your-elderly-parents/

Orford, S. (2023, July 6). *9 Ways to Set Boundaries as a Caregiver.* Healthline. https://www.healthline.com/health/ways-to-set-boundaries-as-a-caregiver

O'Brien, S. (2018, April 4). *Caring for elderly parents can put a dent in your budget.* CNBC. https://www.cnbc.com/2018/04/04/caring-for-elderly-parents-can-put-a-dent-in-your-budget.html

Park, N., Peterson, C., Szvarca, D., Vander Molen, R. J., Kim, E. S., & Collon, K. (2014, September 16). Positive Psychology and Physical Health. *American Journal of Lifestyle Medicine, 10*(3), 200–206. https://doi.org/10.1177/1559827614550277

Perry, E. (2022, September 7). *6 Self-Care Tips for Caregivers.* Better Up. https://www.betterup.com/blog/self-care-for-caregivers

Phillips, B. (2023, June 19). *What is the Sandwich Generation?* Shield HealthCare. http://www.shieldhealthcare.com/community/caregivers/2023/06/19/what-is-the-sandwich-generation/

Pietrangelo, A. (2020, November 23). *11 Elderly End-of-Life Symptoms: Timeline and Providing Support.* Healthline. https://www.healthline.com/health/elderly-end-of-life-symptoms#symptoms

Quillen, D. A. (1999). Common causes of vision loss in elderly patients. *American Family Physician, 60*(1), 99–108. https://pubmed.ncbi.nlm.nih.gov/10414631/

Raypole, C. (2020, October 14). *Losing a Parent: 10 Tips for Handling the Grief.* Healthline. https://www.healthline.com/health/losing-a-parent

Real Simple. (2023, July 17). *Essential Topics You Need to Discuss With Your Aging Parents.* Real Simple. https://www.realsimple.com/health/preventative-health/aging-caregiving/essential-questions-for-aging-parents

Rhodes, L. R. (2023, January 6). *The mental health needs of older caregivers.* Counseling Today. https://ct.counseling.org/2023/01/the-mental-health-needs-of-older-caregivers/

Robinson, L. (n.d.). *The Legacy Conversation: Talking About Funeral Arrangements.* Aging Care. https://www.agingcare.com/articles/funeral-planning-in-advance-149751.htm

Rosenblatt, C. (2013, August 19). *4 Financial Issues You Need To Discuss With Aging Parents.* Forbes. https://www.forbes.com/sites/carolynrosenblatt/2013/08/19/smart-ways-to-talk-to-aging-parents-about-finances/

Rosenblatt, C. (2021a, July 17). *What Makes Aging Parents The Happiest?* Forbes. https://www.forbes.com/sites/carolynrosenblatt/2021/07/17/what-makes-aging-parents-the-happiest/

Rosenblatt, C. (2021b, November 15). *Taking Control Of Finances For Aging Parents: Avoid These 3 Common Mistakes.* Forbes. https://www.forbes.com/sites/carolynrosenblatt/2021

/11/15/taking-control-of-finances-for-aging-parents-avoid-these-3-common-mistakes/?sh=2999da942fad

Rotter, K. (2022, May 18). *Power of Attorney: When You Need One.* Investopedia. https://www.investopedia.com/articles/personal-finance/101514/power-attorney-do-you-need-one.asp#toc-how-a-power-of-attorney-poa-works

Santoro, H. (2022, January 28). When siblings become caregivers. *Knowable Magazine.* https://doi.org/10.1146/knowable-012822-1

Schiltz, R. (2023, September 18). *What To Expect As Parents Age.* Senior Safety Advice. https://seniorsafetyadvice.com/what-to-expect-with-aging-parents/

Schroeder, J. (2017, January 17). *Prepare for These Challenges When Caring for Aging Parents.* Acadviser. https://blog.acadviser.com/prepare-for-these-challenges-when-caring-for-aging-parents

Schulz, R., & Eden, J. (2016, November 8). *Family Caregiving Roles and Impacts.* National Academies Press (US). https://www.ncbi.nlm.nih.gov/books/NBK396398/

Scott, E. (2020, December 13). *How Being a Caregiver Can Be Very Stressful.* Verywell Mind. https://www.verywellmind.com/common-causes-of-caregiver-stress-3144519

Senior Lifestyle. (2020, June 3). *The Mental Health Benefits of Socializing for Seniors.* Senior Lifestyle.

https://www.seniorlifestyle.com/resources/blog/the-mental-health-benefits-of-socializing-for-seniors/

Senior Lifestyle. (n.d.-a). *Caring for Aging Parents Checklist.* Senior Lifestyle. https://www.seniorlifestyle.com/resources/blog/check list-for-taking-care-of-elderly-parents/

Senior Lifestyle. (n.d.-b). *40 Resources for Adult Children Caring For Aging Parents.* Senior Lifestyle. https://www.seniorlifestyle.com/resources/blog/40-resources-for-adult-children-caring-for-aging-parents/

Skwarecki, B. (2018, October 23). *How to Navigate the Health Care System Like a Pro.* Lifehacker. https://lifehacker.com/how-to-navigate-the-health-care-system-like-a-pro-1829920168

Smith, J. (2020, January 31). *How to Navigate the American Healthcare System.* Medium. https://jhsmdconsulting.medium.com/how-to-navigate-the-american-healthcare-system-847dd0a4dddf

Smith, M., Robinson, L., & Segal, J. (2019, January 7). *Coping with Grief and Loss.* HelpGuide. https://www.helpguide.org/articles/grief/coping-with-grief-and-loss.htm

Snowdon, M. (2020, September 8). *Having an emergency fund is a very good idea.* The National Council on Aging. https://www.ncoa.org/article/having-an-emergency-fund-is-a-very-good-idea

Sollitto, M.. (2018, August 23). *Dealing with an Elderly Parent's Bad Behavior.* AgingCare.

https://www.agingcare.com/articles/how-to-handle-an-elderly-parents-bad-behavior-138673.htm

Sullivan, J. (2023, May 10). *How you can benefit from therapy as a family caregiver — and ways to get started.* Care.com. https://www.care.com/c/caregiver-therapy-benefits/

Sumner, C. (2020, June 30). *When Mom Moves in... Key Legal Considerations Before an Aging Parent Moves in with an Adult Child.* JD Supra. https://www.jdsupra.com/legalnews/when-mom-moves-in-key-legal-30304/

Sutton, J. (2018, April 25). *Grief Counseling: Therapy Techniques for Children and Hospice Care.* Positive Psychology. https://positivepsychology.com/grief-counseling/

Taylor, H. (2023, April 26). *How Much Should You Have in an Emergency Fund at 65?* Yahoo Finance. https://finance.yahoo.com/news/much-emergency-fund-65-110016831.html

Taylor, M. (2021, June 21). *What Is an Eldercare Financial Planner and Does Your Parent Need One?* Firstly. https://firstly.com/articles/what-is-an-eldercare-financial-planner-and-does-your-parent-need-one/

Terry, J. (2009, January 1). *Communicating End-of-Life Wishes.* Focus on the Family. https://www.focusonthefamily.com/parenting/communicating-end-of-life-wishes/

The Arbors & the Ivy. (2020, October 14). *Assisted Living Communities Near You in Massachusetts & Connecticut.* Arbors Assisted Living.

https://arborsassistedliving.com/role-reversal-how-to-navigate-becoming-a-family-caregiver-for-an-aging-parent/

Thomas, P. A., Liu, H., & Umberson, D. (2017, November 11). Family Relationships and Well-Being. *Innovation in Aging*, *1*(3), 1–11. https://doi.org/10.1093/geroni/igx025

Trust&Will. (n.d.). *5 Powerful Celebration of Life Ideas to Help Say Good-bye.* Trust & Will. https://trustandwill.com/learn/celebration-of-life

Tugend, A. (2019, November 6). How to (Gently) Help Your Aging Parents Manage Their Money. *The New York Times.* https://www.nytimes.com/2019/11/06/your-money/help-aging-parents-manage-money.html

Tulane University. (2021, March 1). *Why healthcare advocacy is important.* Public Health. https://publichealth.tulane.edu/blog/healthcare-advocacy/

Twin Town Villa. (2021, April 22). *Making the Most of the Time with Your Elderly Parents.* Twin Town Villa. https://twintownvilla.com/quality-time-elderly-parents/

Umberson, D., & Karas Montez, J. (2010, October 8). Social Relationships and Health: a Flashpoint for Health Policy. *Journal of Health and Social Behavior*, *51*(1), 54–66. https://doi.org/10.1177/0022146510383501

VHA Home Health Care. (2022, July 11). *Tips for Talking to Aging Parents About Their Finances.* VHA Home

HealthCare. https://www.vha.ca/news/tips-for-talking-to-aging-parents-about-their-finances/

Wasilewski, M. B. (2020, September 21). *How to share caregiving responsibilities with your sibling(s)*. Your Health Matters. http://health.sunnybrook.ca/wellness/how-to-share-caregiving-responsibilities-siblings/

Webber, T. (2022, March 2). *Setting boundaries as a caregiver is important for you and them*. UK Human Resources. https://hr.uky.edu/thrive/03-02-2022/setting-boundaries-as-caregiver-is-important-for-you-and-them

WebMD. (2001, September 4). *Recognizing Caregiver Burnout*. WebMD. https://www.webmd.com/healthy-aging/caregiver-recognizing-burnout

WebMD. (2008, November 25). *Role Reversal: Caregiving for Aging Parents*. WebMD. https://www.webmd.com/healthy-aging/features/role-reversal-caregiving-for-aging-parents

WebMD. (2018). *Grief: What's Normal? What Are the Common Stages?* WebMD. https://www.webmd.com/balance/normal-grieving-and-stages-of-grief

WebMD. (2021). *What to Know About Cognitive Decline in Older Adults*. WebMD. https://www.webmd.com/healthy-aging/what-to-know-about-cognitive-decline-in-older-adults

Wei, M. (2018, October 17). *Self-care for the caregiver*. Harvard Health. https://www.health.harvard.edu/blog/self-care-for-the-caregiver-2018101715003

Whitley, M. (2021, October 25). *Essential Legal Documents for Aging Parents*. A Place for Mom. https://www.aplaceformom.com/caregiver-resources/articles/essential-documents

Williams, E. (2023, July 28). 5 ways to set boundaries as a caregiver. *The Atlanta Journal-Constitution*. https://www.ajc.com/life/5-ways-to-set-boundaries-as-a-caregiver/OUGTVGCUJBG2NNL6OWBO7QWRV4/

Woodyard, C. (2011). Exploring the therapeutic effects of yoga and its ability to increase quality of life. *International Journal of Yoga*, *4*(2), 49–54. https://doi.org/10.4103/0973-6131.85485

Xu, X. Y., Kwan, R. Y. C., & Leung, A. Y. M. (2019, May 22). Factors associated with the risk of cardiovascular disease in family caregivers of people with dementia: a systematic review. *Journal of International Medical Research*, *48*(1), 030006051984547. https://doi.org/10.1177/0300060519845472

Zamorano, D., & Quezada, A. (2021, May). Effects of role reversal between parent and adult offspring. California State University. https://scholarworks.lib.csusb.edu/cgi/viewcontent.cgi?article=2365&context=etd

Zamorano, D. Z., & Quezada, A. D. (2018, November 28). *How to Handle a Role Reversal With Your Aging Parent*. Companions for Seniors.

https://companionsforseniors.com/2018/11/role-reversal-aging-parent/

Made in the USA
Las Vegas, NV
29 November 2024